Prayer 101

"This book blends biblical principles with a measure of current methodology to form a readable, solid, and practical instruction on prayer."

—Dr. Dan R. Crawford
senior professor of evangelism and mission
Southwestern Baptist Theological Seminary

"Elaine's experience is distilled into this guide for you and your church: practical, simple, and filled with love for the praying believer, and the local church as a house of prayer."

—Dana Olson
director, Prayer First; chairman,
Denominational Prayer Leaders Network

"No book can rise above its author. You can have confidence that you will be reading from one who has walked the path she recommends."

—Dr. John Franklin, president
John Franklin Ministries

"*Prayer 101* is a map to a better prayer life. Elaine uses her experience leading prayer ministries and teaching others to pray, to create a personal prayer primer that can be used by new and experienced pray-ers."

—Jennifer Schuchmann
coauthor, *Your Unforgettable Life*

"The content of this book is rich, informative, and challenging and especially helpful to prayer leaders as a tool for group study on prayer."

—Ann Landry
author and prayer leader, Delaware

"Elaine is making an extraordinary contribution with her work, *Prayer 101*. She writes from experience and practice, rather than mere theory. Your prayer life will be richer from reading this book."

—**Dr. Roy Fish**
retired senior evangelism professor,
Southwestern Baptist Theological Seminary

"This is an excellent tool for individuals and ministry teams. Put this book into the hands of every believer you disciple!"

—**Rev. Phil Miglioratti**
facilitator, National Pastors Prayer Network

"*Prayer 101* combines inspiration and instruction in a manner that gives evidence of the writer's intimate relationship with the Father. Read it with heart wide open."

—**Dr. Gary Frost**
pastor, Evergreen Baptist Church, Brooklyn, New York

"*Prayer 101* 'hits the mark!' It covers more ground than most, yet is one of the most concise I have been privileged to receive and read in three decades . . . imprinted with truth and insight gained only through 'hands-on' experience with Jesus in the place of prayer."

—**Gary P. Bergel**
President, Intercessors for America

Prayer 101

WHAT EVERY INTERCESSOR NEEDS TO KNOW

ELAINE HELMS

NEW HOPE
PUBLISHERS

Birmingham, Alabama

New Hope® Publishers
P. O. Box 12065
Birmingham, AL 35202-2065
www.newhopepublishers.com
New Hope Publishers is a division of WMU®.

Library of Congress Cataloging-in-Publication Data

Helms, Elaine, 1945-
  Prayer 101 : what every intercessor needs to know / Elaine Helms.
    p. cm.
  Includes bibliographical references and index.
  ISBN-13: 978-1-59669-203-9 (sc : alk. paper)
  ISBN-10: 1-59669-203-0
  1. Prayer--Christianity. I. Title.
  BV210.3.H455 2008
  248.3'2--dc22
              2007031148

ISBN-10: 1-59669-203-0
ISBN-13: 978-1-59669-203-9

N084126 • 0414 • .5M2

Prayer of Dedication

Father, I dedicate this book about communicating with You to You with the prayer that it will bring You glory; for You alone are worthy to be praised. Thank You for inviting us into Your throne room and for the privilege of working with You through prayer. Anything good in this book is from You and I submit it back to You for the equipping of the saints for the work and joy of prayer.

May this tool bring an increase to the number of Your children listening to and obeying You; as we grow to love You with our whole hearts and love each other as ourselves. O Lord, please awaken within us a new hunger and desire for more of You, that You might be pleased to revive Your church in our day. For Your glory alone, and in Jesus's name, amen.

In loving memory of my praying parents,
Roger and Mattie Rutland

Contents

Foreword

Are you looking at your church, knowing there must be more spiritual power than you are experiencing? Are you shuddering at the cultural downslide in your neighborhood or city? Are you looking at your personal walk with God, feeling there must be something more He has for you? If so, here is a book that holds many of God's secrets for your church, your community, and for you—an intercessor!

For many years Elaine Helms and I have worked as one in Jesus, spoken together at conferences, traveled and prayed together. I personally have had a full-time prayer ministry for 37 years; and it was so affirming to read the many things we both believe and teach about prayer. But as I read this manuscript, I was pleasantly surprised and challenged when things were covered that God had taught her—not me.

Elaine is extremely qualified to write this book. She developed and ran a very successful church prayer ministry for 14 years. She was the prayer chair for Quest Atlanta '96 to prepare for the World Olympics outreach, 1991–96. During those years, she became active with me in the AD 2000 Women's Track and later became president of our Christian Women United, the American arm of the Women's Track. Moving from the local church to national prayer leadership within the Southern Baptist Convention has expanded her platform for teaching, speaking, and helping facilitate large conferences such as the 150th anniversary of the Fulton Street Revival in New York City.

But in addition to all she has done, I have observed her firsthand through challenges, difficulties, and victories all of these years, and I can attest to her complete trust in God's power and her unequivocal obedience to His leading. So I eagerly recommend these principles to you—an intercessor!

Warning! Before you try to apply this book's teachings, please take the time to thoroughly study chapter 1. Let God speak directly to your heart about all the things He sees that need changing or need to be added for your almost mind-boggling potential power as an intercessor. (In group settings, this may take several sessions.) If necessary, as Elaine explains so well, make sure Jesus is your Lord and Savior. Otherwise, the potential of being a powerful intercessor (one who prays for people and circumstances) will not apply to you. Perhaps you will find yourself going back over this incredibly important chapter many times as new needs surface.

If you are a beginning pray-er, a quick look at the book's table of contents probably will be overwhelming to you. If so, start small with just one thing God is showing you to do. Let the Scriptures, not plans and programs, be His specific advice to you. But most importantly, start praying—not just studying about prayer.

If you are a mature pray-er, let God start with your honest, heart-searching study of chapter 1. Keep open to the Lord's showing you from His Word what you already are doing right and then what practices and beliefs He wants to change. The world of prayer power is open to you, so let Him lead. For instance, if your church does not have a consistent prayer program, perhaps He wants you to help organize a church prayer ministry. Or you might orchestrate studying this book as curriculum in a Sunday School class, a Bible study, or with small prayer groups. This book overflows with fresh ideas for prayer retreats, Bible studies, group and personal praying. There are enough exciting suggestions to keep your prayer life fresh and meaningful for years.

Before you even start to read and apply this book, would you dare to pray this prayer with me?

> *"Oh dear Holy Father: Please remove all my precon-ceived ideas about prayer—whether they are wrong, or whether biblically correct but not applicable for the current time and its needs."*

Then, having let God remove all hindrances, untimeliness, and errors, pray this prayer:

> *"God, now show me the next step in prayer You have for me. I am listening and promise to faith-fully obey You."*

You are now ready to embark on one of the most thrilling adventures of your earthly life with the privilege of coming into the throne room of the Father, engaging in two-way conversation with Him, and then accomplishing His will for Planet Earth through your prayers.

Evelyn Christenson
Chair of the Board, United Prayer Ministry
St. Paul, Minnesota

Foreword

I have had the privilege to know Elaine Helms for many years. We've served together in the area of prayer and I'm excited that she has chosen to impart her knowledge in this work. Here is a thoroughly biblical book on prayer! The basic foundational Scriptures are laid out for the reader. A very comprehensive treatment of the doctrine of prayer is given in easily understood language and exposition.

A practical application is also provided, giving the reader insightful suggestions on how to live out an effective relationship with God in fellowship and prayer. One is encouraged to go on to maturity in prayer with helpful how-to suggestions and experiential testimony. There is even a strong encouragement to add further Scriptures out of the reader's own prayer pilgrimage.

I was honored to direct the Office of Prayer and Spiritual Awakening in Southern Baptist life for many years. In fact, my entire life has been committed to practicing and teaching prayer and intercession. This book is a welcome addition in the area of prayer and one that I will reference through life.

Dr. Henry Blackaby
Blackaby Ministries International
Author of *Experiencing God*

Acknowledgments

I thank God for my husband, Joel, who suggested I submit this book to a publisher. (Thanks, Andrea Mullins and New Hope.) His support and prayers helped me stay the course. Our son, Joel, a Navigators campus minister, gave me insights I found most helpful.

Sincere thanks to the many prayer supporters, including Barbara Clark, Ann Landry, Linda Bemis, Theresea Tipton, Cynthia Castleberry, Bitsy Keith, Phil Miglioratti, Jerry and Debbie Kotyuk, and Gary Bergel. Thanks to the Southern Baptist Convention state conventions, and national prayer leaders' group, PrayerLink, for their prayers dedicating this book to the Lord for His glory.

Thanks to Bryant Wright, our Bible teaching pastor for over 25 years, who inspires us to go deeper with God; to Ted and Suzi Harris, who invited me to Jennifer Schuchmann's journalism group at Johnson Ferry Baptist Church; to all in our small group who studied this material to refine it; and especially to Ty and Dee Gregory, Ed and Suzanne Weiss, John and Julia Jefferson, Don and Nancy Waldrop for prayers and encouragement.

My appreciation to you, reader, for using this book. May God richly bless you as you seek to know Him better through prayer.

Introduction

Does your church offer opportunities or incentives to pray? Jesus said in Mark 11:17, "My house shall be called a house of prayer for all the nations." Does that describe your church? If not, you may be an instrument that God uses to help bring your church into the center of His perfect will.

You may be thinking that you are just one person; but think about Elijah. In James 5:17–18, God tells us that "Elijah was a man with a nature like ours, and he prayed earnestly that it would not rain, and it did not rain on the earth for three years and six months. Then he prayed again, and the sky poured rain and the earth produced its fruit." Have your prayers been answered like that recently?

Since God hasn't changed throughout the ages (see Psalm 102:24–27), when our prayers seem futile, the problem may be that we don't understand His purposes or why God invites us to pray. He explains the breakdown in our understanding in Isaiah 55:8–9: "For My thoughts are not your thoughts, nor are your ways My ways, declares the Lord. For as the heavens are higher than the earth, so are My ways higher than your ways, and My thoughts than your thoughts."

Look back into 1 Kings 17 for more details about all that God accomplished for His glory through the powerful prayer of Elijah referenced above. God told Elijah what He was going to do and how to pray. Elijah was being obedient. God doesn't answer our frivolous prayers so we can impress the crowds, but He does expect us to trust Him and obey when He directs us to pray what is on His heart. What an adventure our Father invites us to enjoy with Him through prayer. God loves to do the things that only He can do—and they often leave us speechless. The disengagement comes when God invites us to pray giant, impossible prayers, but we settle for timid, cautious, and fruitless prayers.

With some basic principles of prayer understood and actions applied to your personal life, you can become an intercessor God hears and answers. *Vine's Dictionary* defines an intercessor as one who seeks "the presence and hearing of God on behalf of others." I have heard the erroneous statement that "everyone knows how to pray, so there's no need for training on prayer." Just as newborn babies do not have meaningful conversations with their parents until they learn to talk, we as Christians do not automatically have meaningful conversations with our heavenly Father until we learn to pray.

Even though the disciples walked with Jesus daily and observed His consistent prayer life with His Father, they still needed more and asked Him to teach them to pray. They knew how to pray, but they noticed Jesus— that prayer was the key to His ministry. They wanted to pray in the way Jesus prayed. Jesus often said that He did nothing of His own initiative, but only as His Father directed Him. He received that direction through prayer, and set the example for us to understand why we need to pray. We need to seek God and His direction through prayer as we strive to be more and more like Jesus.

It is noteworthy that the only thing the disciples asked Jesus to teach them to do was to pray. In Luke 11:2, Jesus began with *"When you pray"* and that tells us that prayer is to be a vital part of our Christian lives. He did not say, *"If you pray."* While it is true that some are more drawn to intercession than others, all Christians are called to pray.

Even if you already have a personal daily prayer time, participate in a small prayer group or a prayer chain, take prayerwalks, or serve in a prayer room at your church, you may still feel like there's more to prayer than you are experiencing. Would you like to go from a dry or feeble prayer life to a growing, active, and powerful prayer life? It is my prayer that reading this book will be of value to you in your quest to grow. To give you an idea of what you can expect, here are some highlights of what is included.

Chapter 1 discusses the why of prayer and our **position for prayer**. For example, a child of the King is heard by virtue of his position as child and heir. Looking at what God had to say when He first created the world offers insight into what God had in mind for our relationship with Him and why He invites our continual conversation with Him, our Creator. In His Word, He gives us very clear guidance for what makes Him listen to our prayers, what hinders our prayers, and the power He has given to us through prayer. God wants us to pray for His glory and for His kingdom to come to earth as it is in heaven.

Before approaching the throne of our holy God, we must be clean. You will better understand confession of sin, cleansing and forgiveness of sin, so that you can turn loose of even the most distasteful of past sins and accept your new righteousness. You'll even learn some of the physical positions or postures of prayer.

Chapter 2 is about the **priority of prayer**. Spending time with the Lover of your soul is not so much a discipline as it is the building of a love relationship, but it does take commitment and time. Having a quiet or dedicated time to be with the Lord will ensure that you get to know Him; so basic principles of developing good prayer habits are covered.

Scripture gives clear guidance about fasting and the importance of incorporating the discipline of physical denial into our lives to show by our actions that God is our priority as we learn to live by the Spirit. Get ready to adjust your priorities when you pray.

Chapter 3 will introduce patterns or what to include in your prayertime and why. **Patterns for prayer** include the acrostics ACTS and PRAY, and the Lord's Prayer. "Praising God Through the Alphabet" is an exercise to increase your awareness of who God is and His many attributes. There is a clarification between praise and thanksgiving. Praise is pleasant both to God and to us; it draws our attention off of ourselves and onto Him.

Just as children learn to talk by repeating their parents' words, we can learn to pray by repeating our Father's words from the Bible back to Him. A key to praying in the character of Jesus is to have a firm biblical foundation for prayer.

Chapter 4 will help you in the important area of **listening to God** and growing in persistence through prayer. Prayer is training for eternity and for the time when we will reign with God. Prayer can be a dialogue with our heavenly Father that can be very edifying if we learn to be still and listen. He answers and gives us wisdom, but He answers in His perfect timing.

God also expects our **obedience** the minute we hear His direction or command; that becomes easier the more we know we can trust Him completely. A sign of our maturity is when God knows He can trust us to obey Him. Learning to wait with persistence for God's answer is sometimes difficult, but a rewarding and necessary part of prayer.

Chapter 5 discusses the **pleasure of prayer**. We can learn to simply enjoy being in the company of our Father who loves us. The more we get to know Him, the more we will embrace the abundant life Jesus came to give us. Journaling can help us remember new insights that God reveals from His Word, and rereading answers to our past prayers builds our faith. Writing expresses thanks to God and gives the glory to Him where it belongs, and also leaves a legacy for future generations. You can solidify your memory of God's faithfulness and gain better understanding as you write and meditate on His Word.

Chapter 6 teaches how to pray and make **supplication** for your personal needs and the needs of others. Some of the areas of praying for provision include the daily bread kind of needs—food, shelter, and clothing, as well as job needs, career choices, and relationships with work associates.

Praying for protection includes health and healing, as well as safety and good judgment. Praying for others includes those in authority (both spiritual and governmental), how to pray for missionaries, how to pray for the salvation of the lost, and how to pray for other Christians.

Chapter 7 explains the relationship of **spiritual warfare** to prayer. It would be unwise to overlook what the Bible says about the warfare we can expect in prayer and how we are to handle it. The uniform for prayer is the whole armor of God and this armor is discussed piece by piece. When we become Christians, we are at once enlisted in God's army, but when we become intercessors, we are sent to the front lines. We need to be ready!

Chapter 8 introduces many ways to **put prayer into action,** both alone and with others. It is important to pray with others in agreement. Jesus gave us a wonderful promise in Matthew 18:19–20, "Again I say to you, that if two of you agree on earth about anything that they may ask, it shall be done for them by My Father who is in heaven. For where two or three have gathered together in My name, I am there in their midst."

Some ideas are suggested for a personal prayer retreat, prayerwalking on your own, and participating in Shield-a-Badge with your church. Ways to pray with others include prayer chains, focused prayer groups, and participating in a church prayer room. You may wonder what goes on in a church prayer room, so highlights of a typical hour in a 24/7 prayer room are covered. How do you pray with someone over the telephone? You will learn some important points to know and remember as you answer any prayerline.

Prayer groups can be small or large at your church or in your community. If you are having trouble finding a group, you'll be interested in the helpful hints for finding or starting one. The idea of praying out loud in a group may have you paralyzed with fear, but with a clearer understanding of the dynamics of group prayer, you will gain confidence to try it for yourself.

Praying with national initiatives includes the National Day of Prayer for America, Day of Prayer for

Revival and Spiritual Awakening, Adopt-a-Leader, See You at the Pole for teenagers, or online initiatives, to name a few.

Conclusion

There is much to discuss about participating in a church prayer ministry. So in response to the need, this was written for Christians who want to grow in their personal prayer lives and be better prepared to participate with others in their churches' prayer ministries. It is my prayer that you will find this book to be a helpful tool as you seek to go deeper with the Lover of your soul. (See Psalm 42:7.) The Holy Spirit is the best teacher of all; and as you study your Bible and rely on Him more and more, you will gain confidence to be the intercessor God intends for you to be.

I encourage you to get your Bible and keep it handy as you read. Where it says to see a certain Scripture, it will be helpful if you read it while you are reading that section. Of course it is always good to check the Bible for yourself to make sure an author has it right. That's biblical and is a good safeguard in reading any Christian book. In Acts 17:11 Luke tells us about the early Christians in Berea: "Now these were more noble-minded than those in Thessalonica, for they received the word with great eagerness, examining the Scriptures daily, to see whether these things were so." Let's get started on this journey into maturity in prayer with our Father in heaven.

CHAPTER 1

Position for Prayer

Have you ever thought that God isn't interested in your prayers because He already knows everything? Or, have you felt inadequate to voice what's on your mind? Our adversary, "the father of lies" (John 8:44), loves to plant doubt in our minds to make us shy away from the intimate love relationship we were created to enjoy with our heavenly Father. That's why it is important in discussing prayer to understand our value to God and His purpose for prayer. Understanding who God is and the position He gives us with Him is a key to developing our love relationship with the One to whom we pray.

Consider the price God paid to reclaim us, to buy back what was His in the first place since He created us. If He didn't care about us, He wouldn't have sent His Son Jesus to become one of us, to suffer ridicule, pain, and the most horrible death known to mankind. Jesus wouldn't have come knowing death was His mission, without a compelling love for His Father and for us to motivate His obedience. Jesus often said that He came to do the will of His Father who sent Him (see John 12:27–28).

If there had been any other way to redeem us, Jesus wouldn't have gone through the emotional pain of being separated from His Father. That period of time when God could not look at Him, because He was carrying our sin, must have seemed like an eternity— evidenced by Jesus's words from the Cross, "My God, My God, why have You forsaken Me?" (Matthew 27:46). To be sure, we don't deserve that kind of extravagant love, but by God's grace and for His purposes He chose to love us and communicate with us through prayer. He assures us, "For I am the Lord your God . . . you are precious in My sight . . . I love you" (Isaiah 43:3–4).

The first step to develop a meaningful prayer life is to know who we are talking with and why He gives us the privilege and responsibility to pray. It's important to know our position—how we are related—or who we are in Christ, and also to understand prayer from God's perspective.

God's Original Plan

Looking at what God had to say when He first created the world gives us insight into what God had in mind for our relationship with Him and for our continual conversation with our Creator. This will help us understand the why of prayer. In Genesis 1:26–28, "God said, 'Let Us make man in Our image, according to Our likeness; and let them rule over the fish of the sea and over the birds of the sky and over the cattle and over all the earth, and over every creeping thing that creeps on the earth.' God created man in His own image, in the image of God He created him; male and female He created them. God blessed them; and God said to them, 'Be fruitful and multiply, and fill the earth, and subdue it; and rule over the fish of the sea and over the birds of the sky, and over every living thing that moves on the earth.'"

God's original plan was for people to be His representatives or ambassadors managing the earth that God had created. God walked and talked with Adam in the "cool of the day," giving him assignments, as evidenced by Genesis 3:8–9. God gave authority to people to be in charge. Adam named the animals and so they are called. When Adam and Eve sinned, they gave up their authority to Satan, the serpent; and that is why the devil could offer Jesus the world in his temptation (Matthew 4:8–9), and why we have evil, sickness, and death in our world today. After the first sin, authority over the earth was handed to Satan. However, God's plan was not foiled.

The thread of redemption runs all through the Old Testament beginning in Genesis 3, as God waited for the fullness of time to bring Jesus as our Savior. Jesus was born as a man so that he could live without sin and be the spotless Lamb of God (John 1:29) to die in payment of our debt. Satan even thought he had won when Jesus died on the Cross, but God raised Jesus on the third day. After many witnesses had beheld His resurrected body (Acts 1:1–3), He ascended into heaven where He sits at the right hand of the Father, making intercession for us (Romans 8:34). He bought back what people had given away.

Why Pray?

When we believe in Jesus for our salvation and ask Him to be Lord of our lives, He gives us back the full authority and right relationship with Him that He originally intended for us to have. In Psalm 115:16, it is repeated, "The heavens are the heavens of the Lord; but the earth He has given to the sons of men." When our eyes are opened to the kind intention of God's will to work through man, the importance of prayer becomes much clearer.

God is not just looking for intercessors; He is searching for those He can depend on to speak on earth what He wants to do. In Ezekiel 22:30 God said, "I searched for a man among them who would build up the wall and stand in the gap before Me for the land, so that I should not destroy it; but I found no one." A good intercessor who understands why God gave us the responsibility of prayer, and is willing to pray, is still hard to find.

God created mankind for fellowship with Himself (prayer) and from the beginning He walked and talked with His people. Biblical examples abound: Adam in the garden, Enosh, when men began to call upon the Lord, Enoch, Abraham, Isaac, Jacob, and Joseph (Genesis 3:8; 4:26; 5:24; 12:1,4; 13:14-17). God continued talking with Moses, Joshua, the judges, and the prophets in the Old Testament.

Jesus walked and talked with the apostles. After He ascended into heaven and the Holy Spirit came to indwell believers, the apostles and early disciples prayed as a lifestyle. We would do well to follow their example. Jesus not only prayed continually during His earthly ministry, "He is able also to save forever those who draw near to God through Him, since He always lives to make intercession for them" (Hebrews 7:25).

Love for God is a big reason to pray. Our conversation with God today—prayer—comes as an overflow of His love for us and our desire to get to know Him and return that love. We pray for direction, too, because God has a purpose for our being here and work for us to do. God gave us prayer to communicate with Him, and God is searching for intercessors.

In obedience to God, we pray. Jesus taught His disciples (including us) to pray by teaching the Lord's Prayer as the way to pray. And in Luke 18:1, He addressed timing. "Now He was telling them a parable to show that at all times they ought to pray and not to lose heart." Protection from evil is a wise and great reason to pray. Jesus warned in Mark 14:38 to "keep watching and praying that you may not come into temptation; the spirit is willing, but the flesh is weak."

Relationships for Prayer

Born again—saved believer

The first step to a relationship with God is of course becoming a saved person or believer. In Hebrews 11:6 God says, "And without faith it is impossible to please Him, for he who comes to God must believe that He is and that He is a rewarder of those who seek Him."

Paul sums up the gospel in 1 Corinthians 15:3–6: "For I delivered to you as of first importance what I also received, that Christ died for our sins according to the Scriptures, and that He was buried, and that He was raised on the third day according to the Scriptures, and that He appeared to Cephas, then to the twelve. After that He appeared to more than five hundred brethren at one time, most of whom remain until now, but some have fallen asleep."

One of the most familiar Bible verses packs the rich doctrine of the gospel in its few words. Jesus was talking to Nicodemus when He said in John 3:16, "For God so loved the world that He gave His only begotten Son, that whoever believes in Him shall not perish, but have eternal life." In verse 3, Jesus said, "Unless one is born again he cannot see the kingdom of God." In 1 John 5:1 we learn, "Whoever believes that Jesus is the Christ is born of God."

If you want to be—but are not sure that you are—a saved individual or believer in Christ, take a moment right now to pray. *Dear God, I know that I am a sinner and need a Savior. I believe that You sent Jesus to be my Savior and right now, I ask You, Jesus, to take control of my life—to be my Savior and Lord. I repent of trying to live my life my own way and I surrender my life to You. Please take me into Your family and fill me with the Holy Spirit to empower me to live for You alone.*

If you are sincerely praying this prayer for the first time, be sure to tell someone very soon about your decision to trust in Jesus for eternal life. Romans 10:9–10 says, "If you confess with your mouth Jesus as Lord, and believe in your heart that God raised Him from the dead, you will be saved; for with the heart a person believes, resulting in righteousness, and with the mouth he confesses, resulting in salvation." You can now embrace the abundant life Jesus came to give.

We no longer have to hope we will go to heaven when we die; we are sure. John, when explaining why he was writing the book, said in 1 John 5:13, "These things I have written to you who believe in the name of the Son of God, so that you may know that you have eternal life."

Child of the King of kings
You may have had a wonderful father who loved you and did most things right as you were growing up, or you may have had a very ungodly father who abandoned or abused you. We all have different life-experiences that can affect the way we relate to our heavenly Father

who loves us. When there is a bad earthly example, that's very bad news. However, the good news is that when we ask Jesus Christ to come into our hearts and to be Lord of our lives, we receive adoption into the family of God—He "shows no partiality" (Galatians 2:6).

Knowing that we are children of the King of kings gives us the assurance that our Father God loves us and hears us at any time. A great promise to us as children of God is found in 1 John 5:14–15. It is one to memorize. "This is the confidence which we have before Him, that, if we ask anything according to His will, He hears us. And if we know that He hears us in whatever we ask, we know that we have the requests which we have asked from Him."

The family relationship gives us rights and intimacy reserved for only that inner circle. We can be ourselves, come to Him in good times and bad, when needy or just reflective. The bond of love between parent and child is demonstrated in our heavenly Father's love for us. "See how great a love the Father has bestowed on us, that we would be called children of God; and such we are" (1 John 3:1).

As children of God we are also heirs. What a legacy this is, but Romans 8:15–17 also alerts us to the suffering that goes with our legacy. "For you have not received a spirit of slavery leading to fear again, but you have received a spirit of adoption as sons by which we cry out, 'Abba Father!' The Spirit Himself testifies with our spirit that we are children of God, and if children, heirs also, heirs of God and fellow heirs with Christ, if indeed we suffer with Him so that we may also be glorified with Him." Suffering can be expected, but it pales in light of our future glory with Christ.

Friend of Christ

When Jesus was talking to the disciples and explaining the relationship we have to Him as His followers, He said in John 15:13–15 (italics added), "Greater love has no one than this, that one lay down his life for his *friends*. You are My *friends* if you do what I command you. No longer do I call you slaves, for the slave does not know what his master is doing; but I have called you *friends*, for all things that I have heard from My Father I have made known to you."

One of my favorite childhood memories is when my daddy taught me to sing the hymn, "What a Friend We Have in Jesus." The words to that hymn are good prayer doctrine to help us understand that we can take any and everything to Jesus because He is not just our Savior, He is our faithful Friend who is always there ready to listen and handle our burdens. See Matthew 11:28–30 where Jesus invites His friends, "Come to Me all who are weary and heavy-laden and I will give you rest."

Royal priesthood

Another important relationship to mention is priest. In Revelation 1:5–6 we learn, " [Jesus] loves us and released us from our sins by His blood, and He has made us to be a kingdom, priests to His God and Father." Isaiah 61:6 says, "You will be called the priests of the Lord." Peter agreed that God has special work for us as priests to do and says in 1 Peter 2:5, "You also, as living stones, are being built up as a spiritual house for a holy priesthood, to offer up spiritual sacrifices acceptable to God through Jesus Christ."

What are some of the spiritual sacrifices that we as priests are to offer? In Psalm 50:14, Scripture says, "Offer to God a sacrifice of thanksgiving." Sometimes we just don't feel grateful, and begin to dream of more that we want. That's when thanksgiving is a sacrifice to self and a good time to remember to thank God for the blessings He has already given to us.

Romans 12:1 says, "Therefore I urge you, brethren, by the mercies of God, to present your bodies a living and holy sacrifice, acceptable to God, which is your spiritual service of worship." Taking care of our bodies by eating healthy, exercising, being pure and undefiled in our actions are acts of worship that we as priests are to perform. God cares about our physical bodies as well as our minds. We as priests are to be holy as God is holy (see 1 Peter 1:15).

Being a good priest of the Lord includes the sacrifice of good stewardship. Paul tells us in Philippians 4:18 about sacrificial giving by the church of Philippi that provided for his needs and was "a fragrant aroma, an acceptable sacrifice, well pleasing to God." In our own strength we struggle with sacrifice, especially praising God when our circumstances are difficult; but God even supplies what is needed so that His priests can offer Him praise. Hebrews 13:15 says, "*Through Him then*, let us continually offer up a sacrifice of praise to God, that is, the fruit of lips that give thanks to His name."

Priests in the Old Testament offered lambs and other animals as sacrifices. But today God calls us to be His priests—continually offering to Him the costly sacrifice of holy living.

God's fellow workers

Jesus performed many miracles of feeding thousands, healing people, and restoring sight; He even raised Lazarus from the dead. Amazingly He tells us in John 14:12 that through our belief in Him, we also will have power to accomplish amazing things for the Father's glory. "Truly, truly, I say to you, he who believes in Me, the works that I do, he will do also; and greater works than these he will do; because I go to the Father. Whatever you ask in My name, that will I do, so that the Father may be glorified in the Son."

When He was alive on earth, Jesus could only preach to so many people at a time in order to invite them to believe in Him. Now that He is in heaven and we have the Holy Spirit, we, His church, can do greater works because we can tell many millions about Jesus and the good news of salvation. That is a greater work we get to do with our Father, telling others about the love of our life—Jesus.

God intends for us to work with Him and calls us His fellow workers in 1 Corinthians 3:9. Paul tells us in Ephesians 2:10, "For we are His workmanship, created in Christ Jesus for good works, which God prepared beforehand so that we would walk in them." How can we know what the good works are? Through Bible study and prayer, as we spend time with the One in charge, we get our directions from God for the work that He wants us to do. He is seeking obedient workers.

What Makes God Listen?

In His Word, God gives us very clear guidance for what makes Him listen to our prayers. Our Father God desires our fellowship so much more than we do and is waiting eagerly for us to call unto Him. In Jeremiah 29:12–13, God reveals the importance of having an undistracted heart to be heard when He says, "Then you will call upon Me and come and pray to Me, and I will listen to you. You will seek Me and find Me, when you search for Me with all your heart." In Psalm 145:18, God emphasizes the importance of truth. "The Lord is near to all who call upon Him, to all who call upon Him in truth." In Jeremiah 33:3, He promises, "'Call to Me, and I will answer you, and I will tell you great and mighty things, which you do not know.'"

Prayer begins and ends with God

An important biblical principle of prayer is that prayer was God's idea—prayer originates with God. He initiates or prompts us to pray, He equips and empowers our prayers, and then He answers. He is training us for eternity. He invites us into partnership with Him to implement His own decisions in the affairs of mankind. God often explained what He was going to do, then let His people ask for it. In Ezekiel 36:37, after God told of the blessings He planned to bestow upon Israel, He said, "Thus says the Lord God, 'this also I will let the house of Israel ask Me to do for them: I will increase their men like a flock.'"

God is sovereign and makes it clear that He is in control. In Isaiah 46:9–10, God says, "I am God, and there is no one like Me. . . . My purpose will be established, and I will accomplish all My good pleasure." God's plans will go forward with or without us. If we disobey or don't respond to His promptings for action, He will use someone else. We will miss the blessing, but God's purpose will be accomplished.

God uses our prayers to accomplish what He wants to do, or in some cases to prevent judgment. In Ezekiel 22:30, God said, "I searched for a man among them who would build up the wall and stand in the gap before Me for the land, so that I would not destroy it; but I found no one." God was talking about Jerusalem and His desire to find one person to stand in the gap for its defense. One person obedient to God can make a difference.

The first of many examples of God initiating intercession was when He appeared to Abraham by the oaks of Mamre in Genesis 18. Read verses 17–19 to hear the thoughts of God before He talked with Abraham about Sodom and Gomorrah. When the men went toward the cities, the Lord stayed before Abraham as if to say, "Do you have anything to ask?" God prompted Abraham to intercede on behalf of Sodom and Gomorrah and was willing to spare the city if only ten righteous men could be found. God's heart is redemption not destruction.

One man, Moses, interceded and prevented God's judgment and wrath against the children of Israel. They had begun to worship the golden calf while Moses was on the mountain with God in Exodus 32. God saw from His vantage point and declared to Moses, "Now then let Me alone, that My anger may burn against them and that I may destroy them." However, Moses responded by interceding for the people and pleaded in verse 12, "Turn from Your burning anger and change Your mind about doing harm to Your people." Again God revealed His heart for redemption and not destruction in verse 14, "So the Lord changed His mind about the harm which He said He would do to His people." One man's prayers made a difference.

God not only wants to listen to our prayers, He invites us to come to Him with even the most impossible requests. "'Present your case,' the Lord says, 'bring forward your strong arguments'" (Isaiah 41:21). The big question is not, "Does God listen to our prayers?" The more poignant question is, "Will we speak up about the plight of our fellow man? Will we pray?"

First John 5:14 assures us, "This is the confidence which we have before Him, that, if we ask anything according to His will, He hears us." This verse helps us see the value of reading, studying, and knowing God's Word so that we can know Him and His will. Then our prayer will be in line with His purposes and we can know that He hears and will answer.

For the glory of God

The promises of God are to be understood within the context of the whole Bible. Notice the phrase in John 14:13, "that the Father may be glorified in the Son." Is what we are asking for God's glory? Whatever we need to share our faith, to build up the body of Christ, to do His work, He will provide.

Selfish praying will leave us disappointed, as clearly illustrated in a story B. J. Willhite tells in his book *Why Pray*. He tells about a rancher who hired a man to build a fence on his property. The rancher loaded up the pickup truck with fencing materials and tools and told the hired man if there was anything he wanted, to call him and he would give it to him.

As the hired man worked, he kept thinking about what the rancher had said—if he wanted anything, to call and he would give it. Soon he couldn't stand it any longer and called the rancher. When the rancher asked what he wanted, the hired man told him he wanted a new car. Of course the rancher laughed at such a request; his offer was for anything to complete the job he had hired the man to do.

When we delight ourselves in the Lord, He will give us the desires of our heart (Psalm 37:4). The more we delight ourselves in Him, the more our desires will line up with His heart.

Jesus emphasized in Matthew 6:33, "But seek first His kingdom and His righteousness, and all these things will be added to you."

Yes, Jesus loves to give us blessings we don't deserve; but He is seeking humble, pure, and obedient hearts. When we approach God His way, we can know that He is listening and we can be a vessel He chooses to use. What a privilege to help our Father in His work that will last for eternity!

Power in prayer comes from God

Jesus shared His Father's plan for giving us power in prayer in John 15:7–8, "If you abide in Me, and My words abide in you, ask whatever you wish, and it will be done for you. My Father is glorified by this, that you bear much fruit, and so prove to be My disciples." When we abide with Jesus, surrendering to His authority, we can begin to see what is on His heart.

In John 16:23–24, Jesus also said, "Truly, truly, I say to you, if you ask the Father for anything in My name, He will give it to you. Until now you have asked for nothing in My name; ask and you will receive, so that your joy may be made full." There is power in the name of Jesus and our connection with Him is where we obtain His power. To leave no doubt about the importance of that connection, Jesus clarified in John 15:5: "Apart from Me you can do nothing."

What Hinders Our Prayers?

There are several things that can hinder our prayers, and knowing about them will help us to avoid the traps. There are three main hindrances to being heard and answered in prayer: sin, wrong motives, and unbelief. For a more in-depth study of hindrances, I recommend T. W. Hunt's Bible study *Disciple's Prayer Life,* published by LifeWay Christian Resources.

Sin in our lives will interfere with our communication with God. Isaiah 59:1–2 tells us, "Your iniquities have made a separation between you and your God, and your sins have hidden His face from you so that He does not hear." We'll discuss sin and confession more thoroughly later in the chapter.

Wrong motives may not be obvious to us at first, but God sees our hearts and knows why we are asking Him for something. A good question to ask is, "Why do I want God to answer my prayer?" Will it bring glory to God or is there a selfish motive? James 4:3 says, "You ask and do not receive, because you ask with wrong motives, so that you may spend it on your pleasures."

Unbelief is an inability to know and trust God to be who He says He is. When we trust in our own understanding, we just see impossible circumstances. However, when we trust in God's Word we can have assurance that "nothing is too difficult for [Him]" (Jeremiah 32:17). Unbelief can also be caused by the wrong idea that God does not want to answer. In Ephesians 3:19–21, Paul prays for us that we would know the love of Christ which surpasses knowledge so that we can pray with assurance that God is able. Verses 20–21 are key verses to memorize, "Now to Him who is able to do far more abundantly beyond all that we ask or think, according to the power that works within us, to Him be the glory in the church and in Christ Jesus to all generations forever and ever. Amen."

The power that works within us is the Holy Spirit and we can quench that power by sin in our lives, wrong motives, and unbelief. The choice is up to us. Remember the story of the disciples who were unable to heal a boy brought to them by his father in Mark 9:16–29. The disciples were unable to heal the boy because of their unbelief. When Jesus said to the father, "All things are possible to him who believes," the boy's father cried out, "I do believe, help my unbelief." If you struggle with unbelief, ask God to help you believe; He will.

Confession and Forgiveness—Keys to Fellowship

Forgive others

Jesus said in the model for prayer in Matthew 6:12, "And forgive us our debts, as we have also forgiven our debtors." Notice the past tense; we have forgiven our debtors before we come to ask for forgiveness. That timing is very important as our reconciliation with others carries a lot of weight in the way God looks at our debts.

If we look back in Matthew 5:23–24, Jesus says to be reconciled to our brother or sister before we give our offering to the Lord. That's to the point of leaving it at the altar and going immediately to be reconciled. Again in Matthew 6:14–15, it is very clear that unless we forgive men, our Father will not forgive us. Our fellowship will be broken. We will still be His child, but not a very happy one. Obedience is the smart way— "There's no other way to be happy in Jesus, but to trust and obey" (as written by John H. Sammis and Daniel B. Towner in "Trust and Obey" [*The Baptist Hymnal,* 1991 edition]).

Confess sin and ask for forgiveness

Not only will our failure to forgive others create a chasm, but also sin in our lives will keep our prayers from being heard. Several verses say it best. "Who may ascend into the hill of the Lord? And who may stand in His holy place? He who has clean hands and a pure heart, who has not lifted up his soul to falsehood"

(Psalm 24:3–4). "If I regard wickedness in my heart, the Lord will not hear" (Psalm 66:18). "Behold, the Lord's hand is not so short that it cannot save; neither is His ear so dull that it cannot hear. But your iniquities have made a separation between you and your God. And your sins have hidden His face from you, so that He does not hear" (Isaiah 59:1–2).

It is important to be still before God long enough for Him to search our hearts. As the bright light of the Holy Spirit shines in every part of our hearts, God will reveal those areas that we have grown accustomed to overlooking. Some sins may seem insignificant to us, but to God sin is sin. If you are serious about being clean before God, ask Him to search your heart. Be prepared for grief though as you face the seriousness of your sin. Brokenness over sin leads to repentance and restoration as we confess and God forgives. Then the joy of our salvation returns.

Psalm 51 is the famous prayer of David when he realized his sin of adultery and murder. It is a great model of asking for forgiveness. In verse 10 David prayed, "Create in me a clean heart, O God and renew a steadfast spirit within me."

There is a powerful promise to memorize and believe in 1 John 1:9, "If we confess our sins, He is faithful and righteous to forgive us our sins and to cleanse us from all unrighteousness."

Accept God's forgiveness

Sometimes we find it hard to believe that we are forgiven, but when God says we are, we can cling to that truth. Psalm 32 is a meaningful chapter to help us accept God's forgiveness of confessed sin. Often the devil will put thoughts into our minds to try to persuade us that

God could not have really forgiven us. I encourage you to read all 11 verses. It begins with, "How blessed is he whose transgression is forgiven, whose sin is covered!"

King Hezekiah wrote after his illness and recovery in Isaiah 38:17, "It is You who has kept my soul from the pit of nothingness, for You have cast all my sins behind your back." God Himself promises in Isaiah 43:25, "I, even I, am the one who wipes out your transgressions for My own sake, and I will not remember your sins." Micah 7:18–19 says, "Who is a God like You, who pardons iniquity . . . because He delights in unchanging love. . . . Yes, You will cast all their sins into the depths of the sea.

Thankfully, with God we can have a clean slate—a fresh start—anytime we are willing to confess our sins and repent of going the wrong way. In Psalm 51:7, David prayed, *"Purify me with hyssop, and I shall be clean; wash me and I will be whiter than snow."* Picture a landscape covered with freshly fallen snow and you get an idea of the kind of clean we can know. In Isaiah 1:18, God tells us, *"Though your sins are as scarlet, they will be white as snow."* Let's pray for a spirit of repentance, forgiveness, and snowlike cleansing by God to fall on Christians everywhere.

It is helpful to remember some analogies that God uses to reinforce our understanding of the completeness of His forgiveness. God will not remember forgiven sins— He washes away our sins, He puts them behind His back, and He casts them into the depths of the sea. These are pictorial promises to hold on to in preparation for when our adversary throws the arrows of doubt at us.

Guard your heart

In learning to walk with God, the best guidance comes from Him. He tells us in Proverbs 4:23 (NIV), "Above all

else, guard your heart, for it is the wellspring of life."
When Samuel was explaining to Saul why he would
no longer be king of Israel, he said in 1 Samuel 13:14,
"But now your kingdom shall not endure. The Lord has
sought out for Himself a man after His own heart."
Then when Samuel was seeking the new king to anoint,
he was advised by God in 1 Samuel 16:7, "God sees
not as man sees, for man looks at the outward appearance, but the Lord looks at the heart." Then God chose
a shepherd to be the new king.

We need to be careful what we hear, what we see,
and what we say to develop and maintain a pure
heart. Jesus tells us that our words reveal our character,
as they are an overflow from our heart. In Matthew
12:33–34 He says, "The tree is known by its fruit . . . the
mouth speaks out of that which fills the heart."

If you have a glass of milk on the table and you
bump it, what will spill out? Milk, of course. The question we need to ask ourselves is, "When I am bumped,
what spills out of my mouth?" Is it blessing or cursing?
How is your heart?

There is hope if you have trouble in this area. We
can be made clean by the washing of the word of God.
In Ephesians 5:25–27 we learn that "Christ also loved
the church and gave Himself up for her, so that He
might sanctify her, having cleansed her by the washing of water with the word, that He might present to
Himself the church in all her glory, having no spot or
wrinkle or any such thing; but that she would be holy
and blameless." As we continually feed on God's Word,
our hearts will be changed. Romans 12:1–2 are good
verses to memorize. "Be transformed by the renewing
of your mind."

Maturity is the goal of prayer

The ultimate goal of prayer is to get to the position of mature fellowship with our heavenly Father who loves us so. Ephesians 4:12–16 teaches that our maturity relates to the church and is for the purpose of building up the whole body of Christ. God gives Christians spiritual gifts "for the equipping of the saints for the work of service, to the building up of the body of Christ; until we all attain to the unity of the faith . . . to a mature man . . . we are no longer to be children, tossed here and there by waves and carried about by every wind of doctrine . . . speaking the truth in love, we are to grow up in all aspects into Him who is the head, even Christ" (Ephesians 4:12–15).

The more time we spend in prayer and Bible study getting to know the Lover of our soul, the better our prayertime will be. We'll also be able to recognize our Good Shepherd's voice, as Jesus described in John 10:1–18, and see the activity of God all around us.

How often do we run into the presence of God, rattle off a few self-centered requests, and make a hasty retreat before He even has a chance to trigger our minds with His Word? God loves us as His children even in our immaturity, but He longs for us to grow up in Him and enter into a more meaningful conversation. "And I, brethren, could not speak to you as to spiritual men, but as to men of flesh, as to babes in Christ. I gave you milk to drink, not solid food; for you were not yet able to receive it" (1 Corinthians 3:1–2). Hear the sadness in Paul's tone in talking to immature believers.

"Concerning Him we have much to say, and it is hard to explain, since you have become dull of hearing. For though by this time you ought to be teachers, you have need again for someone to teach you the elementary principles of the oracles of God, and you have come to need milk and not solid food. For everyone who partakes only of milk is not accustomed to the word of righteousness, for he is a babe. But solid food is for the mature, who because of practice have their senses trained to discern good and evil" (Hebrews 5:11–14).

The time is getting short for us to grow up in Christ. Jesus is coming back as the Bridegroom for His bride, the church, and He is looking for an adult Bride. Revelation 19:6–8 paints a glorious picture of our future. "'Hallelujah! For the Lord our God, the Almighty, reigns. Let us rejoice and be glad and give the glory to Him, for the marriage of the Lamb has come and His bride has made herself ready.' It was given to her to clothe herself in fine linen, bright and clean; for the fine linen is the righteous acts of the saints."

Physical Positions for Prayer

God wants us to express our natural emotion in prayer. There will be times of bent-over, anguished weeping, times of standing with joyous shouts of praise, and more times in between. So whether you feel like bowing your head with eyes closed, lying prostrate on the floor, raising your hands and eyes to heaven, kneeling at an altar, or walking while you pray, you can be relaxed and know that God is more interested in your heart's position. Is it clean and humbled before Him? If so, you are in position to pray.

Some physical positions or actions are associated with prayer in the Book of Psalms. David said in Psalm 4:4, "Meditate in your heart upon your bed, and be still." In 22:23, "Stand in awe." In 24:2–3, "Who may stand?" In 28:2, "I lift up my hands toward Thy holy sanctuary." In 28:11, "I shall walk in my integrity." In 32:11, "Be glad in the Lord and rejoice . . . shout for joy." In 38:6, "I am bent over and greatly bowed down." In 43:4, "I will go to the altar of God." In 65:1, "There will be silence before Thee." In 77:1, "My voice rises to God, and I will cry aloud." In 88:13, "In the morning my prayer comes before Thee." In 95:6, "Come, let us worship and bow down; let us kneel before the Lord, our Maker." In 102:4, "I forget to eat my bread." In 119:62, "At midnight I shall rise to give thanks to Thee." In 119:147, "I rise before dawn and cry for help." In 123:1–2, "To Thee I lift up my eyes . . . so our eyes look to the Lord our God."

I can still hear my childhood Sunday School teacher say, "Let's bow our heads and put our hands together so we can say our prayers." That position for prayer teaches an attitude of reverence, directs our attention to God, and is often associated with prayer today. However, there is no one required physical position for prayer. Paul encouraged Christians to "pray without ceasing" in 1 Thessalonians 5:17; so we need to walk and pray, watch and pray, or drive and pray—to make prayer a part of our daily lifestyle.

========================= **Review** =========================

1. What are some reasons why we pray?

   _____

   _____

2. Name four relationships we have with God.
   We are His _____
   We are His _____
   We are His _____
   We are His _____
   In which role do you feel most comfortable?

   _____

   Why?_____

   _____

3. What are some sacrifices we are called to make as
   God's priests?
   Sacrifice of _____
   Sacrifice of _____
   Sacrifice of _____
   Sacrifice of _____
   What does holy living look like and why is it
   costly? _____

   _____

4. What kind of fellow workers is God looking for?

   _____

   _____

5. What makes God listen to our prayers? _____

   _____

6. What hinders our prayers? _____

_____

_____

7. How can we experience the joy of our salvation?

_____

_____

8. What are three analogies God uses to tell us that He forgets our forgiven sins? _____

_____

_____

9. What is the goal of prayer? _____

10. Prayer is God's plan for accomplishing His purposes. Will you be one He can depend on to pray?

CHAPTER 2

Priority of Prayer

Spending time with the Lover of your soul is not so much a discipline as it is the building of a love relationship; but it does take commitment and time, much like scheduling date nights with your spouse. Having a quiet or dedicated time to be with the Lord will ensure that you get to know Him. Be careful not to allow time with God to become a duty or chore that you must check off your list. Think how you would feel if someone you love considered it a chore to talk to you, or spoke only about themselves when they did talk to you. Take a moment to think about your prayer life. Is it all about you?

Quiet-Time Basics

One big difficulty with having valuable, meaningful time with our Lord is that we live in a noisy world. Machines are whirring or blasting, our own music and that from other people's cars or iPods fill the air, televisions and incessant talking are at every turn. Even in nature there are noisy animals like geese honking and dogs barking. No wonder we often feel the need to fill any silence with conversation.

To "be still and know that [He is] God" takes some planning. When you try to pray, do you find yourself distracted by thoughts of things you need to do? That is not unusual given our multitasking pace. You can prepare for your quiet time, though, by having a pad of paper handy for those thoughts you need to remember. Make yourself a note and then go back to giving your full attention to being with God.

Choose a regular place

What is your favorite place in your home? When you have a special guest, which room do you invite him or her into? Think about where you would be most comfortable meeting with God. As you meet Him there, you will begin to associate hearing from God with that place.

In our home, for many years we used our living room for an office and I also used it for my Bible study and quiet times. One night before I went to sleep, I was telling God all about my day. I was on church staff and was very sure that another staff member needed God's attention. I gave Him my list of the ways that He needed to straighten out this young man with whom I was having a difference of opinion. There had been no words, but my heart was set on my viewpoint and the need for God to change my co-worker. I finished my prayer about other aspects of my day and went blissfully to sleep.

About four o'clock in the morning, God awakened me and suggested I meet Him down at "our place." I arose with anticipation to see what He would say. When He wakes me in the night, it is usually a fresh illumination or discovery and better understanding of His Word. I had just recently purchased a new Bible, and as I opened the clean pages, He led me to 1 Peter 2:1, "Therefore, putting aside all malice and all deceit and hypocrisy and envy and all slander"—I was cut to the quick. God had my full attention; it was like He was saying, "If I can just get you to straighten up, your view of the other person will change." He was right and as I looked back into chapter 1, 1 Peter 1:13–22 (italics added) says, "Prepare your minds for action . . . as *obedient children.* . . . 'You shall *be holy for I am holy.'* . . . If you address as Father the One who impartially judges according to each man's work, *conduct yourselves in fear* during the time of your stay on earth . . . Since you have in obedience to the truth purified your souls for *a sincere love of the brethren, fervently love one another* from the heart."

I was very humbled, repentant, and then thankful for a heavenly Father who corrects and lovingly sets me back on course when I get self-righteous. Sometimes having a new Bible helps us hear God more clearly too. In my previous Bible I had underlined verse 2 and may have missed His correction for me in verse 1. Verse 2 is a great one to know, "Like newborn babies, long for the pure milk of the Word, so that by it you may grow in respect to salvation." But God needed me to see and hear what He was saying for this situation. Because I had a regular place to pray, I knew where to go when God awakened me.

Incidentally, as I released my opinion and asked God to love that young man through me, He gave me a sincere love for him and an appreciation for the ministry he is still doing well. God's ways are higher than ours, and for that I'm so glad.

Choose a time

Think about your schedule and when you are at your best. The psalmist gives testimony to several different times of day to pray: "At midnight I shall rise to

give thanks to You" (Psalm 119:62). "I will be satis-
fied with Your likeness when I awake" (Psalm 17:15).
There are many benefits to beginning your day with
Bible study and prayer. It ensures that you won't let it
slip by and God can better give direction for your day
if you start with Him. The more time you spend with
God in a focused fashion, the easier it will be to "pray
without ceasing" (1 Thessalonians 5:17), and allow the
presence of God to be evident to you all through your
day. Whatever time you choose, give it priority and
consistency.

Prepare your prayer place for personal worship
When you have established where you are going to
meet with God, you may want to prepare for your
time by gathering some helpful tools. You won't waste
precious time looking for supplies every day if you
have your Bible, pen and paper, resource books like a
concordance and a hymnal handy. "God is not a God
of confusion but of peace" (1 Corinthians 14:33). "In
the morning, O Lord, You will hear my voice; in the
morning, I will order my prayer to You and eagerly
watch" (Psalm 5:3).

A woman told me that she prepares two cups of
coffee for her time with the Lord to give her a sense that
she is meeting with someone. The more the place you
meet with God becomes a special place, the more you
may find yourself hearing Him say through the words
of a convicting song, "I Miss My Time with You," if you
don't stop when you pass by your place. Of course you
can meet with God anywhere and anytime, so there
may be more than one special place and time where
you meet with Him. That is the ultimate goal—to be
aware of God with you at all times and in all places.

Timing issues

It seems reasonable to set an alarm to arise in the morning to meet with God; and while that is a great idea, I would also suggest that if there is a limit to your time, set an alarm for when you must move on. You won't have to be concerned about the time. Have you ever met with someone who constantly looked at his watch? That can be very distracting. Remember God is more concerned with your desire to be with Him than with how long you stay. Receive His grace and don't be too hard on yourself. A good verse to remember in prayer as well as in life threatening situations is Psalm 31:15: "My times are in Your hand."

Spend time reading the Bible

In learning to walk with God, the best guidance comes from Him, so the best book you can read is God's Word itself. A plan for reading through the Bible can help you get started. Meditate on His Word like a cow chews her cud. "Be diligent to present yourself approved to God as a workman who does not need to be ashamed, accurately handling the word of truth" (2 Timothy 2:15).

As you read the Bible, ask questions like who, what, where, when, and how. Who is speaking? What is happening? Is there an example to follow? Is there sin to forsake? How about a promise to claim? The answers to these questions are good to write down for deeper comprehension.

For example, in Matthew 7:1–2 Jesus said in the Sermon on the Mount, "Do not judge so that you will not be judged, for in the way you judge, you will be judged." What was Jesus saying to His disciples? How does that apply to your life today? Ask God to examine your heart to see if you have a judgmental attitude that you are unaware of and ask Him to change your heart to please Him.

The Word of God is truly a guidebook for living, as affirmed in Psalm 119:9: "How can a young man keep his way pure? By keeping it according to Your word." In verse 105, we hear that "Your word is a lamp to my feet and a light to my path."

Keep a journal

It is helpful in your walk with the Lord to establish a record for thoughts each day. You can write some of what you said to God and what God said to you, along with new insights and commitments. When you keep a log of prayer requests and their answers when they come, your trust in the faithfulness of God will increase. You can praise Him all over again too when you reread it. Psalm 77:11 says, "I shall remember the deeds of the Lord; surely I will remember Your wonders of old." The value of journaling—recording what God tells us and how He has answered prayer—will be discussed with more detail in chapter 5.

Memorize Scripture

Using a computer, you can only retrieve information that has been stored or programmed. The same is true for what we have available in our memory banks for God to use at the right times in our lives. If we memorize Scripture, it will be available for the Holy Spirit to prompt us to use in resisting temptation, as well as in situations of sharing our faith. "Your word I have treasured in my heart, that I may not sin against You" (Psalm 119:11).

Jesus said that knowledge of His Word is the key to freedom, that "if you continue in My word, then you are truly disciples of Mine; and you will know the truth, and the truth will make you free." He also said that having His Word within us precedes our bearing fruit and proving to be His disciples (John 15:7–8).

Knowing the reference is important when learning Scripture so that you can easily take someone to the written Word of God to let them see for themselves that what you are quoting is from the Bible. God's Word is powerful, He says in Isaiah 55:11, "So will My word be which goes forth from My mouth; it will not return to Me empty, without accomplishing what I desire, and without succeeding in the matter for which I sent it." It is truly the living Word of God.

"All Scripture is inspired by God and profitable for teaching, for reproof, for correction, for training in righteousness; so that the man of God may be adequate, equipped for every good work" (2 Timothy 3:16–17).

One time when I was leading a prayer retreat, I used Scripture but failed to include a reference. At the break, missionary Margaret Burks, who had invited me to speak, reminded me that both she and I knew what I'd said was in the Bible, but the listeners may not know where to find it. I needed to give the verse's address too. I had never thought of the reference being called the verse's address, so that reminder has stuck with me through the years.

The early Christians in Berea "received the word with great eagerness, examining the Scripture daily to see whether these things were so." That's an important reminder to search the Scripture for ourselves to be sure that what we hear preached or taught is being accurately handled and not watered down from the truth.

If you spend much time in the Word, you may be surprised at how much is in your memory. Soon you will begin to recognize the context, the subject, who is talking, or where verses are found in the Bible. See "Memorizing Scripture" in the appendix for some suggested memory verses and advice for effective memorization.

Prayer conferences can be helpful to our growth

Dr. Peter Lord spoke at a prayer conference and had quite an impact on church members related to their quiet times. Sara shared that she had been serious about prayer and a daily quiet time for almost 25 years, but her prayer life had become more perfunctory and obligatory than exciting.

During the conference, Dr. Lord was used by God to renew her passion for a daily communication with Him. She began to use Dr. Lord's loose-leaf notebook, "The 29:59 Plan," and that renewed her desire to pray in more specific ways. A critical lesson she learned was that to truly desire a relationship with God, we must seek His face and not His hand—love God for who He is, and not just for what He can do for us. Sara began to see the benefit of seeking God, praying, and studying His Word—she was being conformed to His image.

As you have opportunity, attend prayer conferences so that you can learn from others who are further along on the spiritual path to maturity in Christ. Even if growth seems like a slow process, God is faithful and rewards even our smallest efforts with His grace. God provided a way to save us because He desires fellowship and communion with us.

Keep circumstances in perspective

A pastor, Colie Rock, used an illustration I'll never forget. He held a hymnal up to his face and said, "When this hymnal is this close to my eyes, it is the biggest thing in the room." However, when he moved it back down to table level, it went back into perspective. The same is true of our circumstances. When we spend time focusing on God, He helps us to see whatever crisis we find ourselves in through His eyes.

A favorite chorus of mine is "Turn your eyes upon Jesus." The words remind us that when we focus on Jesus, the problems and concerns of earth grow "strangely dim" in the light of His glory. When we are focused on our Lord in praise first, it is truly amazing how the burden and size of our crisis—what we had thought so life-threatening—seems to diminish. God is in control and is never surprised by our circumstances. He is the same in good times and bad; so it is very important not to allow our circumstances to blind us to His sovereignty and availability. He has the answer to any problem and tells us to cast all our cares and anxieties on Him because He cares for us (see 1 Peter 5:7 and Philippians. 4:6–7).

Fasting

Fasting is a natural part of a healthy prayer life. It is a way to humble ourselves before God, leaning on Him for strength and denying our physical desire for food. It is giving up something we like, such as sleep, to spend the night in prayer, or solid food, to drink only water or juices for a period of time. It can even be fasting from a favorite activity such as watching TV. The object is to teach our bodies to obey our spirits, not the other way around.

Jesus warned us to watch and pray for "the spirit is willing but the flesh is weak" (Mark 14:38). We should trust in God's care for our physical needs as we seek a deeper relationship with Him. The whole purpose of fasting is to devote the time usually allotted to food preparation, eating, or other activities to God.

When we get so caught up in spiritual things that we no longer worry about what we will eat, then we're becoming more like Christ. Remember in John 4 when Jesus stopped by the well in Samaria and the disciples went to buy food. By the time His disciples returned, Christ had a new convert and had lost His hunger. His reply was, "I have food to eat that you do not know about. . . . My food is to do the will of Him who sent Me" (John 4:32, 34).

Fasting is personal, because Jesus knows the motive of the heart. Fasting to impress others or to try to manipulate God will be a waste of time. However, there is biblical basis and merit in a called corporate fast. One such memorable example is Esther before she went into the presence of her husband, the king, on behalf of her people. In Esther 4:16, Esther said, "Go, assemble all the Jews who are found in Susa, and fast for me; do not eat or drink for three days, night or day. I and my maidens also will fast in the same way. And thus I will go in to the king, which is not according to the law; and if I perish, I perish." God blessed the fasting and prayers of His people and gave a glorious ending to the story.

Fasting as a nation was often done during Old Testament days, and Christian leaders today continue to call God's people to fast and pray during times of decision, danger, and for revival of our love for God. Fasting, along with our prayers for lost people to turn to God, demonstrates the seriousness of our desire for the outcome.

Practical tips for fasting

When you begin fasting for the first time, try skipping one meal, then gradually move to longer periods of time. The longer the fast, the more certain you need to be that it is God who is calling you to fast. In obedience to Him, you will find strength even for 40 days.

Bathe and dress normally when you fast. After giving the model for prayer in Matthew 6:16–18, Jesus gave directions for fasting. "Whenever you fast, do not put on a gloomy face as the hypocrites do, for they neglect their appearance so that they will be noticed by men when they are fasting. Truly I say to you, they have their reward in full. But you, when you fast, anoint your head, and wash your face so that your fasting will not be noticed by men, but by your Father who is in secret; and your Father who sees what is done in secret will reward you."

The Jewish model for fasting was to begin a fast by skipping the evening meal and avoiding food until the following evening. Use the time normally spent eating to read your Bible and pray. Get plenty of rest and drink lots of water. Avoid caffeine and carbonated drinks. I suggest that, as your body learns to follow your spirit's lead, you can make fasting a weekly exercise or extend your fast for several days.

Ending the fast is as important as beginning. Eat very lightly when you end your fast so that your digestive system can begin to function properly again. Drink juices and eat yogurt, fruit, and vegetables. Avoid meat for a few days.

Making prayer a priority includes giving it priority over eating, sleeping, and other physical desires. Developing a regular time with our loving Father, though, is time well spent and the foundation for building a powerful prayer life, both personally and corporately.

"It is necessary for the Spirit of God to burn into
   our hearts this mystery,
That the most important work we have to do is
   that which must be done on our knees,
Alone with God, away from the bustle of the
   world and the plaudits of men."

O. Hallesby

Review

1. What is the primary reason you pray? _____
_____

   Do you think of prayer as building a love relationship with God? _____

2. Name three helpful tools to keep handy in your
   place of personal worship. _____
_____

3. What are good reasons for memorizing Scripture?
_____
_____

   Which verse will you memorize today? _____

4. When circumstances seem to overwhelm us, what
   is the best thing to do? _____
_____

5. What does fasting with prayer demonstrate? ____
_____
_____
_____

CHAPTER 3

Patterns for Prayer

What do you talk about when you first meet someone new? It can be helpful to think beforehand about some topics to get a conversation started. Much in the same way, it is helpful to think about what to include in your prayertime. How should we approach a holy God?

God tells us to love Him with all our minds, so ordering our prayers with some thoughtful planning is a good idea. When asked what the greatest commandment was, Jesus answered in Matthew 22:37, "You shall love the Lord your God with all your heart, and with all your soul, and with all your *mind*" (author's emphasis).

Acrostics: ACTS and PRAY

Patterns for prayer can be helpful in learning to talk to God, and include acrostics like ACTS (standing for Adoration, Confession, Thanksgiving, and Supplication), or PRAY (standing for Praise, Repentance, Asking, and Yielding). In addition to these acrostics, the Lord's Prayer provides a powerful pattern, since it was given by Jesus to His disciples.

There are some common elements in all three of these patterns. Whether you call it praise or adoration, beginning with a focus on the Creator of the universe is the place to start. We become like what we worship, so keeping our eyes on Jesus as we pray will draw us closer to Him. Getting to know the names and attributes of God will help us know what our objective is in becoming more Christlike.

Confession and repentance are contained in both of the acrostics and are present in the Lord's Prayer. To maintain a healthy relationship with God, we must keep short accounts both with Him and with our fellowman. Like spiritual breathing, exhale sin and inhale a refilling of the Holy Spirit. Receiving God's forgiveness makes it easier to forgive others when they step on our toes.

Patterns for prayer are useful in teaching us the important elements of prayer. Praise doesn't seem to come naturally, so we need to learn to praise God for who He is. In order to be in right relationship with God and to be heard by Him, we must confess our obvious and known sin. It is wise to invite the Holy Spirit to search our hearts too. Psalm 19:12 says, "Who can discern his errors? Acquit me of hidden faults." In Psalm 139:23–24, David invites God, "Search me, O God, and know my heart; try me and know my anxious thoughts; and see if there be any hurtful way in me, and lead me in the everlasting way."

Allow your experience with God to be natural

Beginning with praise and adoration of God, it is easier to see our need for confession. Forgiveness leads to thanksgiving and our conversation just flows naturally. Acrostics are only guides to help us develop meaningful prayer; they are not meant to make prayer rigid or legalistic. While using a pattern can be helpful, the important thing is to be yourself and be honest with God.

Comfortable with God

The more we get to know the heart of God by spending time in His Word and talking with Him, the more likely we are to recognize the prompting of His Spirit, and the more comfortable we will become in His presence. My husband, Joel, and I have been married for many years and sometimes on long trips we can drive for miles without talking. Just being with someone you love and know well is comfortable. Conversation is great but not always necessary to communicate. We can often anticipate each other's needs or understand the simplest motion.

When God says to us, "Cease striving and know that I am God" (Psalm 46:10), He is inviting us to calm down and settle our mind on Him. Be comfortable just being quiet in His presence. We will miss the best part of our relationship if we don't spend uninterrupted time alone with Him. He's not in a rush; He has all the time in the world—literally.

Think of prayer as talking to someone you love. God desires your fellowship more than you desire His. "The prayer of the upright is His delight" says Proverbs 15:8. We can know that God is listening and has much to say to us. David said with confidence, "The Lord has heard my supplication, the Lord receives my prayer" in Psalm 6:9.

The Lord's Prayer

Jesus set the example and gave a model for prayer
As Jesus walked with the disciples, He modeled a life of prayer. In the Sermon on the Mount recorded in Matthew 5–7, Jesus taught about the kingdom of heaven, including how to pray. In verses 6:5–15, 33; 7:7–8, He gives specific instruction and we can learn much from heeding His words.

Prayer goes through Jesus
Jesus told us a fact that is hard for some to accept, especially in light of the current meaning of the word *tolerance* in our world today. One way and only one God seems so narrow to the world, and yet God in His compassion and mercy provided that one way so that none would perish. When we have Jesus in our heart, we have the way to the Father in prayer. In John 14:6 "Jesus said, 'I am the way, and the truth, and the life; no one comes to the Father, but through Me.'" First Timothy 2:5–6 confirms, "For there is one God, and one mediator also between God and men, the man Christ Jesus who gave Himself as a ransom for all."

Prayer is private conversation with our *Abba* (or Father)
Matthew 6:6: "When you pray, go into your inner room, close your door and pray to your Father who is in secret, and your Father who sees what is done in secret will reward you."

Abba is derived from baby language and was used to address one's father in everyday Hebrew family life. It translates as "Daddy." Jesus addressed God in His prayers as Abba and in teaching the disciples to pray, gave them authority to use the same term. Our adoption as sons and daughters into the family of God is referred to in Romans 8:15, "You have received a spirit of adoption as sons [and daughters] by which we cry out, 'Abba! Father!'"

A big step in learning to pray is to be alone with God and be still long enough to talk to Him and listen to Him through His Word. Jesus certainly modeled this concept in His ministry here on earth, as He would slip away from the crowd to talk with His Father (Mark 1:35; 6:46). He also encouraged His disciples to do the same. In Mark 6:31, "He said to them, 'Come away by yourselves to a secluded place and rest a while.'" We need those times of refreshing in the private presence of our Father.

Prayer involves belief in the One to whom we pray

Hebrews 11:6: "And without faith it is impossible to please Him, for he who comes to God must believe that He is and that He is a rewarder of those who seek Him." When we consider that with a word from His mouth, God created the heavens and the earth and all living creatures including you and me, it's amazing that He would want to talk with us, His created beings, but He does.

Jesus affirms that fact by telling us how much more important we are than a sparrow, and He knows when a sparrow falls. He even knows how many hairs are on our head (Matthew 10:29–31). God loves us with an everlasting love (Jeremiah 31:3) and created us for fellowship with Him (1 John 1:3). In John 16:27, Jesus tells us of our Father's love for us: "For the Father Himself loves you, because you have loved Me and have believed that I came forth from the Father."

Prayer is addressed to our Father

In response to the disciples' request, Jesus shared His model for prayer and it begins by telling us to whom we are speaking. In Matthew 6:9, He begins, "Our Father who is in heaven, hallowed be Your name." Jesus began with "our" Father to remind us that we as His children are related. We are to pray together and pray for one another.

An important purpose of prayer is building a relationship with God our Father. Just as in a human love relationship, when we are in love, the only person we often think about or want to talk to is the loved one. This is the kind of anticipation God desires for us to have as we approach the prayer closet. "I can't wait to talk to You today, God. What more about Yourself will You reveal to me that I haven't known before?"

The priority of prayer is the will of God

Jesus taught about the importance of God's will in the model for prayer by saying, "Your kingdom come, Your will be done, on earth as it is in heaven" (Matthew 6:10). He also gave more insight into our priority for prayer being the kingdom of God first and our needs second in Matthew 6:33 when He said, "But seek first His kingdom and His righteousness; and all these things will be added to you."

When our focus is on God and our delight is in Him, we begin to see our world from His perspective and not from our own self-centered one. He will direct our prayers and often include us in His work here on earth. Remember the promise of God found in Psalm 37:4, "Delight yourself in the Lord; and He will give you the desires of your heart."

Prayer involves asking

Jesus addressed our personal needs and how we should have them met by saying in Matthew 6:11, "Give us this day our daily bread." Jesus told us to ask and James said that we "do not have because we do not ask" in James 4:2. We are to look to God for all our needs and not lean on our own understanding. By asking for our needs to be met by God, we are acknowledging our dependence on Him. That's good for our attitude of gratitude too.

The "daily" in the request is important. God wants daily fellowship with us. I heard Dee Duke share a story about when his uncle would visit. While he was visiting, he would give Dee, his young nephew, a nickel every time Dee stopped playing and came to talk to him. His nephew often sought out this favorite uncle. Someone asked his uncle why he didn't just give young Dee whatever amount he planned to—at once. Dee's uncle replied that his nephew probably would stop coming to talk to him if he did that and he enjoyed getting to know him.

How very much like the small nephew we are. As long as we want something, we pray to our heavenly Father. He loves our fellowship, though, and no doubt longs for the time when we are mature enough to just want to be with Him for His fellowship too.

Ask for forgiveness of your sins and forgive others

Jesus continued in the model for prayer in Matthew 6:12, "And forgive us our debts, as we also have forgiven our debtors." Our forgiveness of others should reflect our own forgiveness by God. Forgiven people forgive others.

If you struggle with unforgiveness of others, it might help to think of all that God has forgiven you, including the sin that separated you from Him prior to your salvation. Recognizing the mercy you have been shown puts the minor offenses, even when they are grievous, in perspective. Holding a grudge only hurts you, so ask God to empower you to turn loose of unforgiveness.

Prayer helps us avoid temptation

Jesus said in the Lord's Prayer, "And do not lead us into temptation, but deliver us from evil." It is important to understand temptation and the part we have in our own temptation to sin. If we have a weakness for alcohol, we should avoid taverns and bars; if gluttony is a problem, the bakery would not be a good place to visit; if adultery is tempting, don't be alone with the opposite sex. Ephesians 4:27 says, "Do not give the devil an opportunity."

James 1:13–14 further explains, "Let no man say when he is tempted, 'I am being tempted by God'; for God cannot be tempted by evil and He Himself does not tempt anyone. But each one is tempted when he is carried away and enticed by his own lust."

An important habit to develop is, "Taking every thought captive to the obedience of Christ" (2 Corinthians 10:5). By an act of our will we can decide to obey God and not dwell on thoughts that would lead us into sin. Replace unholy thoughts with God's word. Read and meditate and ask God for a fresh filling of His Spirit. Recite some of the verses you have been memorizing. Praise causes the devil to flee so worship God and give Him your full attention.

When temptation sneaks up on us, God has given us a lifeline promise in 1 Corinthians 10:13, "No temptation has overtaken you but such as is common to man; and God is faithful, who will not allow you to be tempted beyond what you are able, but with the temptation will provide the way of escape also, so that you will be able to endure it." We need to be quick to take that escape!

Praise is a vital part of prayer

Jesus concludes His teaching in this model for prayer as He began with recognition of God the Father. "For Yours is the kingdom, and the power, and the glory, forever. Amen." God is worthy of our praise in every way. Psalm 145:3 says it so well, "Great is the Lord and highly to be praised." He is everlasting, always was and always will be. He never changes. Let His praise be in your speech continually as is practiced in heaven by the living creatures, "Holy, Holy, Holy is the Lord God, the Almighty, who was and who is and who is to come" (Revelation 4:8).

It is obvious by the way that Jesus emphasized giving the glory to God at the beginning and the end of the Model Prayer, that praise and adoration are vital to a healthy prayer life.

Difference Between Praise and Thanksgiving

There is a difference in praising God for who He is and thanking Him for what He has done. Praise does not seem to come naturally, but it is a great way to get to know God—His names and attributes. For example, today He may be God my healer, and tomorrow He may be God my protector. The more interaction I have with Him, the more He begins to mean to me. What is your favorite name of God? Was there an experience that makes that name more special than some of His others?

Why praise God?

God is worthy of our praise. Revelation 4:11 describes a worship service in heaven, one that never ends. The 24 elders fall down saying, "Worthy are You, our Lord and our God, to receive glory and honor and power, for You created all things, and because of Your will they existed, and were created." David said in 2 Samuel 22:4, "I will call upon the Lord, who is worthy to be praised." Similarly Psalm 147:1 gives more reasons to praise God, "Praise the Lord! For it is good to sing praises to our God; for it is pleasant and praise is becoming."

Praise is the activity of heaven. Just as the elders worship Jesus in heaven (just mentioned in Revelation 4:11 above), the angels also worship as expressed in Revelation 5:11–12, "Then I looked, and I heard the voice of many angels around the throne and the living creatures and the elders; and the number of them was myriads of myriads, and thousands of thousands, saying with a loud voice, 'worthy is the Lamb that was slain to receive power and riches and wisdom and might and honor and glory and blessing.'"

Praise is the total occupation of some in heaven. "And the four living creatures . . . day and night they do not cease to say, 'Holy, Holy, Holy is the Lord God the Almighty, who was and who is and who is to come'" (Revelation 4:8).

God inhabits the praise of His people. Psalm 22:3 says, "Yet You are holy, O You who are enthroned upon the praises of Israel." It is recorded in 1 Chronicles 23:5*b*, 30 that King David set aside an army of 4,000 whose duty was to praise God every morning and evening.

The battle belongs to the Lord

The inspiring story of King Jehoshaphat in 2 Chronicles 20 tells of how God used the praises of His people to win the victory in a very lopsided war. The situation was the time when three nations were joining forces to come against Judah. Verse 3 says, "Jehoshaphat was afraid and turned his attention to seek the Lord, and proclaimed a fast throughout all Judah." The people came together to pray and the king began his prayer with recounting the many ways God had been faithful in the past and praised Him.

Ending his prayer in verse 12 he said, "O our God, will You not judge them? For we are powerless before this great multitude who are coming against us; nor do we know what to do, but our eyes are on You." God answered through one of the priests in verse 15 that the battle belonged to the Lord.

Even before the victory, the people immediately began to praise God. They still had to go out to the battlefield, where the king assembled the praise team and gave them instructions to go out before the army with singing and praising. At the moment they began to praise God, verses 22–23 records, "The Lord set ambushes . . . destroying them completely. . . they helped to destroy one another."

Days of collecting the spoils of war and praising God followed. God was glorified among the neighboring nations as they heard about what God had done on behalf of His people. What a wonderful story illustrating the significance God places on our praise of Him.

Jesus tells us in Matthew 18:20 that He inhabits our prayers, "For where two or three have gathered together in My name, I am there in their midst." Jesus taught us to praise God in our prayers when He gave His disciples the model for prayer in the Lord's Prayer. He includes praise at the beginning and the end of that prayer.

A final reason to praise God is that we become like what we worship, He with whom we spend time, praise, and talk about. About what or whom do you spend most of your time thinking? If we want to become like Jesus, we need to be around Him and meditate on His names and attributes, and begin to talk like Him.

Paul gives a good illustration of the transformation we can expect in 2 Corinthians 3:18, "But we all, with unveiled face, beholding as in a mirror the glory of the Lord, are being transformed into the same image from glory to glory, just as from the Lord, the Spirit."

How do we praise God?

We can praise God as a way of life along with David who said in Psalm 34:1, "I will bless the Lord at all times; His praise shall continually be in my mouth." Just looking around us at the beauty that God has created—the variety of flowers, trees, topography, waterfalls, mountains; the variety of animals, birds, and butterflies—all demonstrate His creativity. If we get too busy to appreciate all God has given for our enjoyment, we may be too busy.

"The heavens are telling of the glory of God; and their expanse is declaring the work of His hands. Day to day pours forth speech, and night to night reveals knowledge" (Psalm 19:1–2).

It is no doubt easier to praise God when things are going great, but we need to praise God in the good times and in the bad. In the good times, we may begin to get arrogant and think that our success, happiness, or any good thing is the result of our own initiative. We need to be quick to give God the praise and the credit for our good fortune.

In the bad times, we can be thankful that we can turn to Him with a heart of praise and cast all our cares on Him. Hebrews 13:15 lets us know that there may be times when we feel reluctant to praise God; sometimes it is a sacrifice. "Let us continually offer up a sacrifice of praise to God."

Praising God Through the Alphabet

This is an exercise to increase our praise of God for who He is and to help us learn His names and attributes. It can help in times of concern, not only to take anxious thoughts to our Father, but it can help us stay focused on Him through the discipline of the alphabet.

Have you ever taken a problem to God in prayer only to take it right back again to continue stewing about it? At some point when I was trying to take my cares back after giving them to Jesus, God prompted me to leave my cares with Him and praise Him instead. He reminded me of the alphabet and I began to praise Him for who He is. When my thoughts drifted back to my concern, it was like God tapped me on the shoulder and said, "You were on G!" On the following page there is a listing of names to help get you started. Use it as a springboard and be creative as you praise the One who created you in His image.

There are many ways to use the alphabet to help you stay on track when you are praising God. You might try to think of many names or attributes beginning with each letter of the alphabet as you come to it. You could praise God by quickly mentioning just one name or attribute for each letter. You could try to think of different names and attributes each day as you praise Him in your private time with Him. What's interesting is that you will begin to notice names and attributes more when you are reading the Bible and that will increase your praise vocabulary too. I invite you to join me now in a prayer exercise for turning loose of anxiety and falling more in love with Jesus.

Father, we love You and want to praise You better, for You are worthy of praise. You are the alpha and omega, the beginning and the end. Our vocabularies are too small to adequately praise You. Please accept our praise as we use the alphabet to help us think of and remember Your names and attributes.

A Lord, You are Almighty God, Adonai, Awesome, Alpha, the Avenger of evil, the Anointed One, Abundant in loving kindness, and the Ancient of Days.

B You are our Beautiful Savior, the Bright and morning star, the Beloved of the Father, the only Begotten Son of the Father, the Bridegroom, You are the Best! The Bread of life.

C You are our Creator, wonderful Counselor, Confidant, Christ, soon Coming King, Comforter, Courageous, You give us courage.

D You are our Deliverer, Defender, Deity, Devoted, Destroyer of evil, Divine, our Dwelling place.

E We Exalt You, You are Everlasting, Eternal, Emmanuel, Extraordinary, Exciting, El Shaddai.

F You are our Father, Faithful and true, Great is Your Faithfulness, You are Forever, our Friend, Famous, Fabulous, my Favorite.

G Your Grace is amazing and sufficient, You are God, You are the Good Shepherd, Gracious, Great, Glorious.

H You are Holy, holy, holy; You are High and lifted up, Honorable, Hallowed be Thy name, You are our Hope, our Help, our Healer, Heaven is your home.

I You are the Incarnate Word of God, the great I AM, Immanuel, Immortal, Invincible, Innovator.

J You are Jesus, Jehovah, Joyful, righteous Judge, Justice is in Your hand, the Joy of the Lord is my strength.

K You are the King of kings, the Keeper of my soul, my Kinsman Redeemer, Thy kingdom come, all-knowing God.

L You are the Lord of lords, the Light of the world, You are Love, Life giver, Liberty, Liberator of my soul, Leader, Lord Most High, Long-suffering.

M Master, How Majestic is Your name in all the earth, You are Mighty, Merciful, Mediator, Marvelous are Your works!

N You are Near, Never-ending, Now, Your Name is a strong tower, Your Name is above all names, You are our Next of kin, Noble.

O You are Omniscient, Omnipresent, Omnipotent, the One and Only God, the Overcomer

P Lord, You are the Prince of Peace, all-Powerful, our Protector and our Provider.

Q You are quick to come to our aid, You Quicken our spirits, You Quiet our anxious thoughts.

R You are our Redeemer, the solid Rock, our Refuge and Rescuer, You Receive our prayers, You are the Rewarder of those who seek You, Revive us, O Lord.

S Thank You for being our Savior, Sovereign Lord, the Same yesterday, today, and forever, You are our Shield and Shelter, Sustainer, Salvation belongs to You, Lord. You are Safety, a Stronghold in times of trouble.

T You are Tried and True, Triumphant, Trustworthy, our times are in Your hands, You have a Terrible swift sword to defeat Your enemies.

U You Understand, You are Undefeated, Unstoppable, and Universal—the same all over the world.

V You are the Victor, Victory in Jesus, our Savior forever, the True Vine, and our Vindicator.

W You are our Wonderful counselor, You are Wisdom, Worthy of our Worship, Your Wrath may soon be kindled, You are the Way and the Way maker.

X You are eXcellent in all Your ways, Your X-ray vision searches our hearts—create in us clean hearts, O God, and renew a steadfast spirit within us.

Y You are Yahweh, we Yield our lives to YOU, we say Yes, Lord, You are the same Yesterday, today, and forever.

Z You are Zion's King, You are Zealous for souls, help us to be Zealous for souls too. You are the beginning and the end, the first and the last. You are all in all, amen.

Scripture

Scripture offers patterns and substance for prayer. It helps us get to know God, and as we focus on Him and read about the holiness of His name, His faithfulness through all generations, His majesty and glory, we begin to align our thinking with His. Even if we don't know how to pray and feel inadequate to approach God, using the Bible is a good place to start. God knows our hearts and He is delighted with the sound of our voices. Proverbs 15:8 says, "The prayer of the upright is His delight." Come into His presence with thanksgiving in your heart for His word to guide you.

With Bible in hand, offer a simple prayer asking God to open your heart to His word and begin to read. A good verse to personalize and pray back to God is Psalm 104:34, "Let my meditation be pleasing to [You

Lord], as for me, I shall be glad in [You]." When you read His Word and pray it back to Him, as if making sure you understood what He just said to you, you will learn His many attributes. You can begin to praise Him for who He is. Make a list of the attributes in just this one chapter. For example, He is *great, clothed with splendor and majesty* (v. 1), *light* (v. 2), *Creator, Sustainer of life, Provider* (vv. 3–31), *makes man's heart glad* (v. 15), *God of order* (vv. 19–20), *wise, owner* (v. 24), *life giver* (v. 30). How many more names and attributes can you find?

There are many prayers in the Bible that you can pray as you are learning to pray in the character of Jesus. For example, if you want to pray for your spouse or loved one, personalize one of Paul's prayers in his letters to the early churches. For example: Try putting that person's name into Ephesians 1:16–19.

> Father, I thank You for _____ and want to be faithful to pray for him or her that You will give _____ a spirit of wisdom and revelation in the knowledge of You. Enlighten the eyes of his or her heart so that he or she will know the hope of the calling You have made in his or her life. Please give _____ a better understanding of the riches of the glory of Your inheritance in the saints, and the surpassing greatness of Your power toward those who believe, in accordance with Your resurrection power—the power that raised Jesus from the dead. Give _____ faith to believe in the mighty power available to us as Your children. Expand his or her vision of Your purposes for him or her; give him or her opportunity to see that mighty power at work today for Your glory.

Follow the example of Jesus as the best pattern for prayer

Following the pattern of Jesus as He modeled a life of prayer, begin to spend blocks of time with your heavenly Father—seek His guidance for your decisions, take your joys and your sorrows to Him, and give Him praise for He is worthy. "He went up on the mountain by Himself to pray; and when it was evening, He was there alone" (Matthew 14:23). "In the early morning, while it was still dark, Jesus got up, left the house, and went away to a secluded place, and was praying there" (Mark 1:35).

══════ Review ══════

1. Why is it good to begin prayer with praise or adoration? _____

   _____

2. What gives us the right to talk to our Abba Father? _____

3. "And without _____ it is impossible to please Him" (Hebrews 11:6).

4. An important purpose of prayer is _____

   _____

5. The priority of prayer is _____

6. What does it mean to take every thought captive to the obedience of Christ? _____

   _____

7. What is the difference between praise and thanksgiving? _____

   _____

   _____

8. Do you think using the alphabet to learn the names
   of God will help you get to know Him better?
   _____ How will you use it? _____

   _____

CHAPTER 4

Persistence and Listening in Prayer

God is the same yesterday, today, and forever, so He still speaks to His children who persist in prayer, who are willing to be still long enough to hear and obey Him. Listening to God is a vital part of prayer, since prayer is a dialogue with our Father and not a monologue where we do all the talking. Sometimes He speaks through His Word as we are reading the Bible and we suddenly see something we never noticed before, or He draws us to a particular verse. Through the practice of His presence with us, we can learn to recognize His voice in our daily lives, even when we're not reading the Bible.

Jesus talked with the disciples during His earthly ministry and before His crucifixion He comforted them upon the sad news that He was leaving. He explained how He would still communicate with them, and us, when He went back to the Father. In John 16:7–15, Jesus said, "But I tell you the truth, it is to your advantage that I go away; for if I do not go away, the Helper will not come to you; but if I go, I will send Him to you. . . . I have many more things to say to you, but you cannot bear them now. But when He, the Spirit of truth, comes, He will guide you into all the truth; for He will not speak on His own initiative, but whatever He hears, He will speak. . . . He takes of Mine and will disclose it to you."

God Speaks Through the Living Word

It is so encouraging to know that God has not taken a hands-off attitude toward us, His created ones. He is very actively involved in the daily affairs of mankind. In Psalm 81:13, we can hear the heartbreak of a speaking Father, "Oh that My people would listen to Me."

When the Holy Spirit guides us into all the truth, He takes the Scripture we are reading and applies it to us personally where we are while reading it. When He speaks what He hears in heaven, it is a fresh word for us today. I have been amazed when God has brought a Scripture to my memory just as I was in a conversation and that Scripture was needed to point my listener to Him. So it is not only as we are reading, but He may use Scripture that we have memorized for a timely word.

In his book *The Pursuit of God*, A. W. Tozer wrote about the importance of our accepting the Bible as the "living" word of God. He said:

> "I think a new world will arise out of the religious mists when we approach our Bible with the idea that it is not only a book that was once spoken, but a book which is now speaking. The prophets habitually said, 'Thus *saith* the Lord.' They meant their hearers to understand that God's speaking is in the continuous present."

Are You Listening?

Pastor Bryant Wright often asks, "Are you listening?" during his sermons to be sure the congregation catches the important point he is about to make. Jesus often said, "He who has ears to hear, let him hear."

The better we get to know our Father by spending time with Him, the easier it is to recognize His voice. When Jesus said that His sheep recognize His voice, He is letting us know that there will be other voices that will try to get our attention. Certainly God speaks to us in many ways and about different topics; but it is a trustworthy statement that He will never say anything to us in prayer, or through others, that is contrary to His Word. That's why it is so important to read and study the Bible.

One test to find out who is talking is to ask if what you are hearing is conviction or condemnation. Conviction of sin comes from our Father to restore us to Him, but condemnation about past forgiven sin is from our adversary to crush our spirit and defeat us. "Beloved, do not believe every spirit, but test the spirits to see whether they are from God" (1 John 4:1).

Testimonies of Hearing God

When I was a church prayer coordinator, I invited the members of the prayer ministry to come together occasionally for intercessor meetings. I find it encouraging and faith-building to hear how God is working in different people's lives; and we grow in our own prayer lives when we are exposed to the ways of God. A dynamic team spirit seemed to develop, too, when we came together to pray and brag on Jesus. On one of these occasions the topic being discussed was listening to God. I shared the following story with the group.

I remember being at my grandparents' home one stormy evening when my daddy was in Korea with the army. Mother was getting ready for us to go home when my granddaddy stopped her and asked that we stay a while longer due to the storm outside. My uncle Troy started playing the piano and we were all glad we stayed for the singing.

It wasn't until we got in the car and started down the street that we realized how glad we were. There was a huge tree lying across the street where it had fallen during the storm. It gave us cold chills to think that the tree could have killed us if we had been on the street when it fell. God had prompted my granddaddy to save our lives. God was speaking and I'm very glad my granddaddy was listening.

God knows what's best and we can trust Him when He speaks. As I told the story of this incident, we discussed that neither my granddaddy nor his daughter-in-law, my mom, understood at the time why she should wait, they just each obeyed the authority of the one saying wait. That was enough. "But as for me, I trust in You, O Lord, I say, 'You are my God.' My times are in Your hand'" (Psalm 31:14–15).

Listening and obeying promptings

Bitsy Keith shared another illustration of obeying the prompting of the Holy Spirit even though she didn't understand why at the time. They had become temporarily lost in an area of town that they knew quite well. As they would soon learn, God had allowed this to happen for a very good reason. Her husband, daughter, and she had a mission that Sunday afternoon. They had a list of nursing homes to visit in an effort to find one suitable for her dad who recently had a stroke and needed round-the-clock care.

As they approached a large intersection a few blocks off the square in Marietta, Georgia, they noticed a woman, probably in her 70s, walking between the railroad tracks. She had her head down as if looking for something. At first glance, it didn't seem unusual, but something told them to watch her. "Listen, O daughter, give attention and incline your ear" (Psalm 45:10).

So they turned onto the street that ran along the railroad tracks and slowed down to observe her more closely. The woman seemed very slow and unsteady so they turned around and drove back. Bitsy got out of the car, walked up to the edge of the tracks, and yelled, "Can we help you?" She looked up and yelled back, "Maybe so."

With that, Bitsy stepped onto the tracks to assist her. She asked the woman if she lived close by and she began to talk about living in South Carolina and seemed disoriented. She held an empty milk carton in one hand and a piece of paper in the other, and it was obvious that she did not know where she was. However, she agreed to let the Keiths drive her home, wherever that was.

She took Bitsy's arm, and slowly walking off the tracks and up to the car, they heard a loud whistle. They all looked up as a train raced by on the tracks where they had been standing two minutes before. In shock, her husband, daughter, and Bitsy stared in disbelief with their mouths wide open. "He sets the needy securely on high away from affliction. . . . The upright see it and are glad" (Psalm 107:41–42).

Cynthia, they later learned, did not even notice what had happened. Driving up the street they saw a sign that read, *Personal Care Home*. They inquired within and found out that Cynthia had arrived at the home the day before but had not yet received the electronic bracelet to alert the staff if she exited the house. Fire laws prohibit the doors of the house to be locked.

She had probably been gone for about an hour and had not yet been missed.

They said their good-byes to their new friend, who by now had captured their hearts with her sweet spirit. They will never forget Cynthia. She will always remind them that God can use us anywhere, anytime if we listen to and obey that still, small voice of prompting.

"My sheep hear My voice"

Cynthia was a wandering sheep and God used another of His sheep, Bitsy, who by practice recognized His voice, to rescue her from danger. God calls us His sheep in Psalm 95:7–8, "For He is our God, and we are the people of His pasture and the sheep of His hand. Today if you would hear His voice, do not harden your hearts." The love Jesus has for us comes through so clearly in His calling us His sheep in John 10. The Good Shepherd is the door of protection for us in verse 7. He is the way to salvation in verse 9; and in verse 11, He says, "I am the good shepherd; the good shepherd lays down His life for the sheep." He further states the fact that He willingly gave His life for us; He had the authority to lay it down and also to take it up again. In verse 27, we are assured that if we belong to Him, we, like Bitsy, will be able to hear Him clearly. "My sheep hear My voice, and I know them, and they follow Me."

Our present relationship and eternal security make persisting in prayer—listening and obeying—worth our attention. Jesus tells us we can count on Him to hold on to us, no matter what storm or trial we face. In John 10:28–30 He continues, "And I give eternal life to them and they will never perish; and no one will snatch them out of My hand. My Father, who has given them to Me, is greater than all; and no one is able to snatch them out of the Father's hand. I and the Father are One."

Protection through listening

Sylvia Sacia excitedly shared a story that showed tremendous growth in her ability to hear the Good Shepherd's quiet voice of protection. She was driving and planning to turn left, so she got into the left turn lane to wait for the green arrow. When the light turned green, her natural instinct was to quickly make that turn. However the Holy Spirit prompted her to wait a moment. As she hesitated she wondered if it was just her imagination, but in a split second, a car raced by before her eyes, going at least 60 miles an hour through the red light. She would have been killed for sure had she entered that intersection as usual. She was so thankful to God for His constant concern for her. He is prompting; let us cultivate sensitivity—are we listening?

"For the Lord gives wisdom; from His mouth come knowledge and understanding . . . then you will discern righteousness and justice and equity and every good course. For wisdom will enter your heart and knowledge will be pleasant to your soul; discretion will guard you, understanding will watch over you to deliver you from the way of evil" (Proverbs 2:6–12). This list of benefits makes it very worthwhile to listen to God—wisdom, knowledge, understanding, discernment, direction, discretion, and protection from evil to name a few.

Listening for work assignments

Listening to God is not just for our protection. God has work for us to do and when our ears are tuned to hear His voice, He will prompt us to speak a word of encouragement, do a random act of kindness, to be generous when a need is expressed, or to share our faith with someone.

I travel a lot and one day I was at the airport standing near the gate waiting to load a plane. I noticed a very polished, well-dressed woman also standing there. God began to prompt me to speak to her, but I felt awkward and ill-equipped to do so.

After several minutes of contemplation, I felt like I would break out in a cold sweat if I didn't do something, so I hesitantly walked closer to her and said hello. Much to my surprise, she responded warmly, almost thankfully. We began to exchange small talk about where we were going. I revealed that I was in ministry, and soon the call came to load the plane.

As we found our way to our seats, amazingly we were assigned seats next to each other and continued our conversation. After we had settled in for the flight, she began to confide that she was ready to throw in the towel of her faith in God. It suddenly became clear that God needed to place a Christian next to her for His purposes, and it must have been important that I show interest in her prior to our sitting down next to each other. I was able to encourage her while listening to her story, and help her remember that God is still on His throne and not surprised by her circumstances. We were able to pray together and her faith was strengthened.

God has plenty of work available for us to do every day, so we need to be ready for action when we sense Him prompt us. It is good to ask God in the morning to give you an opportunity to work with Him during the day. He will definitely answer that prayer. The question then becomes, "Will we hear Him and obey?"

Another time I was traveling coast to coast and had a briefcase full of work that I hoped to accomplish, while I had a long span of time on my hands. My seat was one of the inside seats in the middle section with five seats. I wasn't thrilled over that seat, so when a mother and adult daughter boarded and were assigned to the seats on either side of me, I offered to trade seats with the one on the aisle. Amazingly she agreed and I settled in with my work in front of me.

However, God had other plans. Almost immediately "Miss Chatty" next to me started asking questions. When she asked where I was going, I responded that I was going to a prayer summit. Well, now I had her interest and the questions increased. "What is a prayer summit?"

I told her it was a time for prayer leaders to come together for four days just to pray. "Pray for four days?" she exclaimed. "How can you do that?" I told her a little about what I expected the experience to be like and said to her, "It's interesting that God is leading you to ask spiritual questions. Do you know Him?" She didn't answer my question, but she admitted after a fair pause, "I guess I am asking spiritual questions."

She then began to tell me about her experience in the church and why she had left it. Then her daughter joined in the conversation to tell me her spiritual background too. Several hours later they both prayed to ask Jesus into their hearts for a real relationship instead of their previous experiences of religious rituals only. We had a little prayer meeting right there on the plane and then my new friends became my sisters in Christ. They gave me their names and addresses so that I could look for a Bible-teaching church in each of their cities to refer them to.

Listening to God and obeying what He says to do ensures that our lives will never be dull. Whether He is protecting us in the face of danger, asking us to be an encouragement to someone else in the body of Christ, or giving us work to do that will last for eternity, our time will be well spent. We get a glimpse of God's glory when we realize we are in His presence and that He is working right where we are. That alone is a good reason to actively learn to listen. For a more detailed teaching on how to learn to hear God's promptings, I recommend Peter Lord's book, *Hearing God.*

God Answers Prayer

No

When we pray according to God's will in the name and character of His precious Son, Jesus, we know that He hears us. First John 5:14–15 tells us so. The more important question is, "Do we hear Him when He answers our prayer?" When He responds to our prayers He either says, yes, no, or wait. For example, prayers for healing can be answered yes with physical healing, and temporary extension of our mortal lives, or with complete healing of a believer who gets to go ahead to be with Jesus. However, we tend to think of death as a no answer. In chapter 6 we will look more fully at how to pray for personal needs.

God is a protective Father; so when we ask Him to give us or do something for us that would bring us great harm, in His love and wisdom, He says no. It is a good practice to ask God to help us see our request through His eyes, so that we can adjust our prayer to get back in line with His will and purposes. There is a good reason when God says no.

Wait or persist

In Luke 18:1–8 we can learn from Jesus Himself about the importance of persisting in prayer. "Now He was telling them a parable to show that at all times they ought to pray and not to lose heart. . . . Will not God bring about justice for His elect who cry to Him day and night? . . . I tell you that He will bring about justice for them quickly. However, when the Son of Man comes, will He find faith on the earth?"

The wait answer can be the hardest for us to accept, especially living in this instant generation—having to wait for 60 seconds in front of a microwave can seem endless! One day I experienced this more clearly. Everything said *wait* that day. Just as I was ready to leave the house for a meeting, the air conditioning service man arrived in my driveway, blocking me in. When I called the doctor's office, I was put on perpetual hold with recorded messages saying, "Thank you for calling. We will be with you soon to give you our undivided attention."

At the copier there was a line of people in front of me also waiting to use it. Running late in leaving the office, I went through the usual procedures to log off my computer but the screen kept the message "Please wait while your computer shuts down" for an extremely long time, although it usually whizzes past that screen. As I finally walked down the hall to exit the building, I passed the sign used prior to our contemporary service and read, *Worship prep in progress, Please Wait.*

It seemed that everything said to wait that day, and I think God was reminding me through the circumstances that He often says wait. It's not the answer to prayer that we want. Even a no is definite and something we can adjust to, but wait puts us in limbo. How do you plan when you don't know the answer?

I remember when my husband, Joel, was on active duty in the army, and he was up for promotion to lieutenant colonel. The months before the promotion came through were like years. Many questions couldn't be answered, like: "Will we still be at the same address in six months?" "Therefore, wait for Me, declares the Lord" (Zephaniah 3:8).

Just as we teach our small children to wait sometimes in order to teach them self-control, God puts us in a wait position to teach us to trust Him. His timing is perfect and He knows best. Micah 7:7 teaches the correct response well: "But as for me, I will watch expectantly for the Lord; I will wait for the God of my salvation. My God will hear me."

Waiting helps us learn to rest in God's promises. I love the story of Elijah in 1 Kings 17–18 and in James 5:17–18. Elijah was prompted by God to pray for drought—"neither dew nor rain" for three years. God met all of Elijah's physical needs during those years of drought as he waited, and even worked several miracles on his behalf. He was fed by a raven and drank from the brook; the widow's bowl of flour was not exhausted; he raised her son from the dead; and he confronted the false prophets on Mount Carmel. (Read 1 Kings 18:7–14 for the humorous exchange between Elijah and Obadiah before the mighty miracle at Mount Carmel.)

When he prayed for rain at the end of the three years, he was filled with faith and waited patiently for the rain to come. He knew when to run too! (Read about him outrunning the king who was in a chariot in 1 Kings 18:46.) I often think of Elijah when I read Isaiah 40:31: "Yet those who wait for the Lord will gain new strength; they will mount up with wings like eagles, they will run and not get tired, they will walk and not become weary."

God wants us to learn persistence in our praying and sometimes makes us "wait" to strengthen our faith. He may have some work to do in our lives before we are ready for the answer. Whatever He says, we can trust that He knows best and His ways are definitely higher than ours.

Yes

Too often when God answers our prayer with a yes, we take it for granted and even think He didn't have anything to do with it. It is important to pray specifically so that we will recognize the specific answer and be quick to give Him the glory for what He is doing in our lives. Thanking God for answering our prayers is good for us; it establishes a healthy attitude of gratitude and increases our awareness of God at work. As our faith grows, we will recognize the work of our Father all around us and praise Him even more.

Obeying God

Spending time in God's Word helps us get to know Him and to understand the limits and the boundaries He has put in place to protect us. Praying or talking with our heavenly Father develops trust. The more we trust and obey Him, the more He will be able to trust us to help Him in His work.

My military father used to explain to my sister and me how very important immediate obedience was to the soldiers during World War II. Their very lives depended upon it. He required the same from us as small children in many situations when we lived in Korean War-era Japan and postwar Germany. I'm thankful for the training he gave us. He told us there would be times when we needed to obey and not ask why, because there would be no time for explanations. He would know the reason; we could trust him and that would have to be enough. That needs to be our response to God. I have often heard Henry Blackaby say, "The moment God speaks to you is the very moment God wants you to respond to Him."

In John 14–15, Jesus explains how very much He and our Father want us in their fellowship and in their family. He knows what is best and we can trust Him. He gave us the free will to choose. The big question is, will we obey?

We show our love to God by our obedience. Our fellowship with Him is related to our willingness to obey Him. In John 14:21, Jesus teaches, "He who has My commandments and keeps them is the one who loves Me; and he who loves Me will be loved by My Father, and I will love him and will disclose Myself to him."

Jesus gave us boundaries to protect us and to provide an abundant life. We can avoid all manner of trouble and difficulty in life by obeying His commands. They are for our good. Jesus clarified why He gave us commandments to obey, in John 16:1. "These things I have spoken to you so that you may be kept from stumbling."

Being Quiet Takes Practice

Listening to God, rather than doing all the talking, is an important lesson we all need to practice in prayer. There's a reason that God created us with two ears and only one mouth. Our tongues can get us into trouble quickly, but seldom does being quiet take us there. Proverbs 17:28 says, "Even a fool, when he keeps silent is considered wise. When he closes his lips, he is considered prudent."

Ecclesiastes 5:1–2 offers some helpful advice in the area of listening to God. "Guard your steps as you go to the house of God and draw near to listen rather than to offer the sacrifice of fools; for they do not know they are doing evil. Do not be hasty in word or impulsive in thought to bring up a matter in the presence of God. For God is in heaven and you are on the earth; therefore let your words be few."

Psalm 12:6, "The words of the Lord are pure words," sums it up, so it makes sense to listen when we come to the place of prayer. God has much to say to us if we will, by training our ears to hear, listen to Him. He loves the sound of our voices, though, so don't stop talking to your Father who treasures you and your visits with Him. Just remember to balance your prayertime to listen to what He has to say too. God is speaking—are you listening, and will you wait on Him?

"So I say to you, ask and keep on asking, and it will be given to you; seek and keep on seeking, and you will find; knock and keep on knocking, and it will be opened to you" (Luke 11:9 AMP).

Review

1. What is the phrase that Jesus often used about listening? _____

   _____

2. What are some ways we may hear God? _____

   _____

3. What does waiting on God help us learn? _____

   _____

4. What are three ways God answers prayer? _____
_____

5. Why does God answer our prayers with no? _____
_____

6. What is the danger we need to avoid when God answers yes?_____

7. Why did God give us commands? _____
_____

8. What does God expect us to do when we hear His command? _____

CHAPTER 5

Pleasure of Prayer

When you think of prayer, do you associate it with pleasure? Too often we pray when we are in trouble, in pain, or when we need something. A sign that you are maturing in your faith is when you desire to be in the presence of the Lord just to be with Him, to ask what is on His heart, or just to rest in His arms in peace and delight. Isaiah 56:6–7 says, "Every one who keeps from profaning the sabbath and holds fast My covenant; even those I will bring to My holy mountain and make them joyful in My house of prayer." When we obey God, He gives us the pure joy of being in His presence.

God created us for fellowship with Him, and the more we get to know Him and grow in our relationship with Him, the more we will spend time with Him just for the pleasure of His company and the joy of working with Him. It is good for us to seek His face to adore Him, not just use prayer to ask for what we want.

God is so loving and generous, though, that we cannot imagine all that He intends to give us (see Ephesians 3:20). "How precious is Your lovingkindness, O God!

And the children of men take refuge in the shadow of Your wings. They drink their fill of the abundance of Your house; and You give them to drink of the river of Your delights" (Psalm 36:7–8).

God tells us in Zephaniah 3:17 (NIV), "The Lord your God is with you, he is mighty to save. He will take great delight in you, he will quiet you with His love, he will rejoice over you with singing." Isaiah 62:5 says, "As the bridegroom rejoices over the bride, so your God will rejoice over you."

Embracing the Better Life Jesus Gives

Jesus said about His sheep, His followers, in John 10:10, "I came that they may have life and have it abundantly." In *The Message,* the same verse says, "I came so they can have real and eternal life, more and better life than they ever dreamed of." Are you experiencing that kind of life with Jesus?

Paul understood the abundant life and is such a good role model for experiencing joy even in times of tribulation. While he was imprisoned, he wrote, "Rejoice in the Lord always; again I will say, rejoice." In Philippians 4:4–13, he gave us the secret for receiving God's peace that passes all understanding—"Be anxious for nothing, but in everything by prayer and supplication with thanksgiving let your requests be made known to God" (v. 6). He gave the formula for keeping our thoughts pure, he exemplified contentment with little or with much, and he explained that living the abundant life is possible only through the strength Christ gives.

David painted a picture of our childlike relationship with God in Psalm 131: "O Lord, my heart is not proud, nor my eyes haughty; nor do I involve myself in great matters, or in things too difficult for me. Surely

I have composed and quieted my soul; like a weaned child rests against his mother; my soul is like a weaned child within me."

Do you remember childhood days when someone older and wiser provided for all our needs, protected us from harm, and all we had to do was obey their rules? Those were happy, carefree days with no worries; we who were cared-for children were secure and at peace within the boundaries of our parents' care.

When Jesus was teaching about anxiety in His Sermon on the Mount in Matthew 6:25–34, He told us that God, our heavenly Father will provide for all our needs and we just need to obey His command to seek first His kingdom and His righteousness. We can again enjoy the carefree joy of being a child—a child of the King.

Glimpses of God's glory

The best part of the abundant life with Christ is that as we mature by practicing our faith and studying His word, God will reveal more about Himself and give us glimpses of His glory. Moses spoke with God in the cloud on Mount Sinai and received the Ten Commandments. By that time he had matured in his relationship with God, and Moses pleaded in Exodus 33:18, "I pray You, show me Your glory!" God explained that humans cannot see the face of God and live, but because He loved Moses, He allowed him to get a glimpse of His glory. God responded in verses 22–23, "And it will come about, while My glory is passing by, that I will put you in the cleft of the rock and cover you with My hand until I have passed by. Then I will take My hand away and you shall see My back, but My face shall not be seen."

David expressed the exuberance he felt when he got a glimpse of God's glory in the wilderness of Judah. Psalm 63:2 in *The Message* says, "So here I am in the place of worship, eyes open, drinking in your strength and glory. In your generous love I am really living at last! My lips brim praises like fountains, I bless you every time I take a breath; my arms wave like banners of praise to you."

Imagine how Peter, James, and John felt when Jesus took them with Him to the mountain to pray, and while He was praying His face and clothing became white and gleaming. "Now Peter and his companions had been overcome with sleep; but when they were fully awake, they saw His glory." (Read the whole story of the transfiguration in Luke 9:28–36.)

Hear the awe in Peter's voice when he tells about that experience in 2 Peter 1:16–18, "We were eyewitnesses of His majesty. For when He [Jesus] received honor and glory from God the Father, such an utterance as this was made to Him by the Majestic Glory, 'This is My beloved Son with whom I am well-pleased'—and we ourselves heard this utterance made from heaven when we were with Him on the mountain."

When we see a life that is changed in a radical way—going from being lost and in darkness to being redeemed and brought into the light, we get a glimpse of God's glory. Glorious change like that only comes by the Spirit of the living God, our life giver (see Colossians 1:13–14). God is at work all around us, doing things that only He can do, so we need to be quick to share "God stories" to bring glory to His name. What a blessing to be given spiritual eyes to see the glory of God in our world today. What a joy to work with our Father by praying the prayers He wants prayed to accomplish His plans. Now that's the abundant life and the pleasure of prayer.

Benefits of Journaling

Have you ever been reading your Bible and see something that you had never noticed before? Suddenly you understand what God meant and how it applies to you at this particular time. It is exciting! While at the time you think you will never forget what you just understood clearly, if you don't write down what you just sensed that God indicated through His Word, and what it meant to you, you most probably will forget about it. Also writing to reinforce your memory of hearing from God will help in learning to recognize His voice. Our memories are flawed, especially today with so much information clamoring for our attention.

I have been so annoyed with myself in just such an incident. I can remember my past excitement over a fresh discovery of truth, but can't remember exactly what it was that was so exciting, or where in the Bible I saw it. In contrast, I have been so encouraged when I have reread a journal entry and been reminded of, and refreshed by, a meaningful truth that I had lost sight of for a time.

When I feel down and like I'm all alone in my trial, I can pick up my journal and be reminded of, and refreshed by, God's faithfulness in the past. Resolve returns, confidence in God builds, and I am able to go the distance and stand firm. In Habakkuk 2:2, God says, "Record the vision and inscribe it on tablets that the one who reads it may run." Sometimes the one who reads it is the one who wrote it, and it inspires us to continue in stronger faith.

Digging deep into God's Word offers insights into who He is. In order to develop a close relationship with anyone, it takes time to talk with and listen to that person to get to know him or her. It is the same with our relationship with God. If we are willing to take the time to be still long enough to hear Him, we will be amazed at all He will teach us.

As we ask for the Holy Spirit to make us aware of truth, the Bible takes on new meaning. Our Father has great plans for our lives and wants us to mature in our faith in Him. That's why journaling is so important to help us remember. We can also write down the prayers we are praying, specific requests and concerns, then record the answers we see coming from God. The following are some specific benefits.

Solidifies memory of God's faithfulness

Expressing our thoughts onto paper reinforces the memory and keeps it alive so that there's less chance that we will forget what God has said or done. "This will be written for the generation to come; that a people yet to be created may praise the Lord" (Psalm 102:18).

Builds our faith

When our defenses are down and we feel weak, the adversary will beat against our resolve to stand firm. That's when an energy boost from rereading the great works of God will come in very handy. "And without faith it is impossible to please Him, for he who comes to God must believe that He is and that He is a rewarder of those who seek Him" (Hebrews 11:6). Faith grows by being tested, so know up front that our faith will be tested. That is a big reason that God wants us to remember all that He has done.

Expresses thanks to God

By the very act of writing out our thankfulness to God, we are thanking Him. When we reread what we have written, we can thank Him again. "Ascribe to the Lord, O sons of the mighty, ascribe to the Lord glory and strength, Ascribe to the Lord the glory due His name" (Psalm 29:1–2).

Gives God the glory

Writing down the insights and answers we receive from God helps us give the glory to God where it belongs, instead of thinking that what happened was from our own efforts. Too often the blessings of God that we didn't even ask for are taken for granted. "My glory I will not give to another" (Isaiah 48:11). The act of writing down our praises for God's goodness to us heightens our awareness of His provision and care.

Leaves a legacy

Having a written record of what God has done leaves a wonderful legacy for our children to find after we are gone. "Tell to the generation to come the praises of the Lord, and His strength and His wondrous works that He has done" (Psalm 78:4). They will better understand the depth of our relationship with our heavenly Father and will in turn be strengthened in their own resolve to follow Him.

Clarifies our thoughts

When we tell someone else about what we have seen or experienced, it helps to clarify in our own mind what we think, how we felt at the time, and the significance of our understanding of new insights. Write to God.

Imparts understanding and insight

"Make me understand the way of Your precepts, so I will meditate on Your wonders" (Psalm 119:27). Often just by spending the time to write out the Scripture we are meditating on will help us better understand what we are reading and learning from our Father. "Thy word is a lamp to my feet and a light to my path" (Psalm 119:105). Writing helps us to learn our Father's commands and requirements.

It's therapeutic

A healthy mind is stimulated by the process of ordering one's thoughts before God. "In the morning I will order my prayer to You and eagerly watch" (Psalm 5:3). Counselors who seem to help others the most are the ones who mainly listen to others express their concerns. Jesus is our wonderful Counselor, so take everything to Him in prayer. "This is my comfort in my affliction, that Your word has revived me" (Psalm 119:50).

It's exciting

To see answers we had overlooked before, to gain new insights into our God, to learn more about Him and what His character is like is truly exciting. His mercies are new every morning; great is His faithfulness! Walking with the Lord is never dull and keeping notes along the way will inspire enthusiasm at how God's timing turns out to be perfect every time.

Prepares us to share with others

The practice of putting on paper the details of what we have seen God do or new insights He has given improves our ability to say things in an understandable way. As we remember something and write it out to get the facts straight, it's amazing how the order and significance of parts of the story need to be rearranged to make better sense to someone else. Ask God to give you insight as you write so that you can see it from His perspective and be better prepared to share His love with another person.

Second Corinthians 1:3–4 says, "Blessed be the God and Father of our Lord Jesus Christ, the Father of mercies and God of all comfort; who comforts us in all our affliction so that we will be able to comfort those who are in any affliction with the comfort with which we ourselves are comforted by God."

Peter also reminds us to be ready to share our faith in 1 Peter 3:15. He says, "Sanctify Christ as Lord in your hearts, always being ready to make a defense to everyone who asks you to give an account for the hope that is in you, yet with gentleness and reverence." The best way to be ready with our testimony is to take the time to write it out—a short and a long version. As you experience God in your daily life, you will have many testimonies about His goodness and love.

How should a journal be used?

You can use a simple spiral-bound notebook to get you started with journaling. As you have prayer concerns such as decisions to be made, illnesses, family needs, names of people who need salvation, relationship problems, and others:

1. Write down the request as you pray to God.
2. Date the request and leave room across the page for answers.
3. Persevere in prayer.

Spend much time in God's Word getting to know Him. He will direct your prayer. As you see God at work, write down:

107

1. What He has made known to you
2. How He answered a specific request

A noticeable way to see God at work through a journal is to write requests in blue or black ink. Then write answers and new insights in red ink. The important things will stand out.

The benefit of having no dated pages is to avoid unnecessary guilt. So often when we start something new, we are too hard on ourselves if we miss a day. If you do miss a day, just get back on track the next day. Journaling is a lifestyle change and like any new habit will take time to develop.

God loves us and wants our fellowship with Him to be joyous and filled with anticipation as we approach Him. Simply date your entries and over a period of time you will see how consistent your walk is becoming. If you desire to see God at work, He will give you the desires of your heart.

My prayer for you is that your journal will become one of your most treasured books as you create a record, a remembrance of God's activity in your life. A journal can be a good record of the pleasure you begin to take in your love relationship with your heavenly Father.

"The Spirit of prayer will not only show you the true meaning and purpose of prayer; He will also lift you in all your helplessness up to the very heart of God where you will be warmed by His love, so that you can begin to pray according to His will, asking for nothing except those things which are in harmony with His plans and purposes."

O. Hallesby

"My prayer life must be brought entirely under the control of Christ and His love. Then, for the first time, will prayer become what it really is, the natural and joyous breathing of the spiritual life, by which the heavenly atmosphere is inhaled and then exhaled in prayer."

Andrew Murray

Review

1. How can prayer be a pleasure? _____
_____

2. What is the secret for receiving God's peace that passes all understanding? _____
_____

3. Name the eight things to dwell our minds on in Philippians 4:8. _____
_____
_____
_____

4. How can we get a glimpse of God's glory? _____
_____
_____

5. What are some of the benefits of keeping a journal?
_____
_____
_____

6. Do you keep a journal? _____ What is your favorite reason?_____

CHAPTER 6

Prayers and Supplication

Praying for our personal needs and for the needs of others is an important part of our prayertime. We need to present our requests to God and then trust Him that He will meet our needs. Jesus taught in the Sermon on the Mount that God cares about us and does not want us to be anxious about what we will eat, or what we will wear and compares us to the lilies of the field that are clothed in glorious array. He said in Matthew 6:33, "But seek first His kingdom and His righteousness and all these things will be added to you."

Paul reiterates this same admonition about anxiety in Philippians 4:6–7 when he says, "Be anxious for nothing, but in everything by prayer and supplication with thanksgiving let your requests be made known to God. And the peace of God, which surpasses all comprehension, will guard your hearts and your minds in Christ Jesus." God assures us that He will provide for our needs.

Difference Between Needs and Wants

The real test comes in distinguishing between our needs and our wants. Are we willing to leave our financial status up to God's good pleasure? Can we be content with little or be generous to bless others if we prosper? Jesus speaks of money (or possessions) numerous times because He knows we tend to be selfish and greedy in the flesh. He warns in Luke 16:13, "No servant can serve two masters; for either he will hate the one and love the other, or else he will be devoted to the one and despise the other. You cannot serve God and wealth."

Ask God to search your heart and help you evaluate if what you are seeking will bring Him glory or elevate your social status. James gives good insight about how to pray in James 4:3–4, "You ask and do not receive because you ask with wrong motives, so that you may spend it on your pleasures . . . friendship with the world is hostility toward God." What is your motive?

Jesus taught us to pray, "Give us this day our daily bread," to help us learn to depend upon Him on a daily basis. There was a reason that God gave only enough manna in the wilderness for the children of Israel to eat each day. It would spoil if they tried to hoard it. Our daily habits develop our character, so we need to practice daily dependence on God. What do you need today? Our Father is ready to respond to our prayers for our daily needs.

Job Needs

Career

Finding or keeping the right job or career can be very time-consuming and thought-monopolizing. If you are successful, it is easy to think that your power and strength made you wealthy, but God gives us a stern reminder in Deuteronomy 8:18, "But you shall remember the Lord your God, for it is He who is giving you power to make wealth." God provides for us in all areas of our lives and wants us to remember that He is the one blessing us. We are His stewards since He owns everything and is allowing us to use it freely. We should be serving Him with all that He gives us. He blesses us to be a blessing to others.

When we pray for ourselves or for others in the area of finding a job, job security, or career choices, we need to keep this in mind. Pray for the person needing a job to seek God's choice and how God can be glorified by the work they do.

One of the intercessors serving in the prayer ministry when I was the coordinator sent me a letter telling me about all that he learned as he waited patiently for God to answer his prayers for a job promotion. His letter illustrates several points, so I want to share it with you.

Dear Elaine,

Two years ago in a sermon around New Year's Day, Thad Smith challenged those in attendance to ask God to do something in our lives, so that when it happened, we would know God made it happen.

At that time in my career at Delta Air Lines, I was in the Airport Customer Service Division, supervising a team of 75 men and women. This allowed me to influence their lives in a significant way and provided me with many opportunities to express my faith. I was beginning to be considered for promotion to the position of duty manager. While this would be the normal career progression, I was uncertain as to whether this was where God wanted me to be, and where I could serve Him best.

At about that time I was encouraged by a Christian friend to interview for a position within the company in Flight Control. It was a job that I very much desired. While I had an excellent record and a broad experiential background with the company, I really didn't think I had a chance of being considered. I knew that I could not obtain this position without the direct intervention of God.

Our pastor, Bryant, frequently says that God is not interested in our wish list. He wants us to seek Him and His perfect will for our lives. So I prayed that morning that God would show me the direction that He would have me go in my career with Delta Air Lines; that He would place me in the position where He desired for me to be and where I could serve him best. If that was Flight Control, only He could make it happen. I asked that if it were His will for my life, He would open the doors and make it happen.

At about this time, in one of Jerry and Laurel Maxfield's Sunday School lessons, they covered 1 John 5:14–15, "This is the confidence which we have before Him, that, if we ask anything according to His will, He hears us. And if we know that He hears us in whatever we ask, we know that we have the requests which we have asked from Him."

On my next off day, I knocked on the door of the director of Flight Control to introduce myself and tell him of my desire to work in his department. This began a process of four interviews and testing that would last over two years. There were months between each. All the while I continued to pray and trust that if it was God's will, He would make it happen. During this process, He was teaching me that our timetable for things happening doesn't always match His. After all, His timing is perfect.

As the time seemed to drag between each interview, I often became discouraged, but I continued to pray. In a subsequent Sunday School lesson, we covered Jeremiah 29:11, "For I know the plans that I have for you, declares the Lord, plans for welfare and not for calamity to give you a future and a hope."

The words jumped out at me. It was as if the Lord was speaking directly to me. I was anxious before each interview and I prayed that God would lead me in knowing what to say. I would repeat the words that Mark Cottingham and the sanctuary choir sang in the musical *God with Us*: "Be strong and take courage. Do not fear or be dismayed, for the Lord will go before you and His light will light the way. Be strong and take courage, do not fear or be dismayed. For the One who lives within you will be strong for you today."

I had asked a number of Christian friends to pray for me about this matter. I will never forget the response of a young Christian man on my team named Darrell when I asked him to pray for me as I was about to go for my final interview. He told me not to worry, that the job was mine. He said that God had set the job aside for me, that I only needed to continue to trust Him and go in and possess it. This sounded very similar to what we were currently studying in Sunday School, in the Book of Joshua, as the people of Israel prepared to cross the river Jordan and enter the Promised Land.

I went to the final interview with a great sense of peace and confidence that, regardless of the outcome, God would place me where He wanted me to be. Some two weeks passed and very early one morning, as I was sleeping in on a day off, the phone rang. It was the director of Flight Control calling. He told me I had been selected for one of the seven positions from over 2,700 people considered. I was being offered the opportunity to become 1 of just over 200 dispatchers for Delta Air Lines and one of some 2,000 in the entire world. As I hung up the phone, I thanked God and opened my Bible. It fell open to Psalm 143:8 (NIV), "Let the morning bring me word of your unfailing love, for I have put my trust in you. Show me the way I should go, for to you I lift up my soul."

The following Sunday, our lesson in the Book of Joshua covered how the Lord had instructed the people of Israel to step out in faith, even though the river Jordan was at flood stage. And when they did so, He dried up the river so they could cross over to the Promised Land. As I sat in that classroom and reflected on what had transpired in my career, I read Joshua 4:24 (NIV), and several of the words stood out to me. "*He did this* so that all the peoples of the earth might know that the hand of the Lord is powerful and *so that you might always fear the Lord your God.*"

Once again, God had spoken to me. He has continued to bless me on this journey. I ask you

to continue to pray for me that I would measure up to the enormous responsibility with
which I have been entrusted, and that I would
be salt and light to those I come in contact with
as I attempt to glorify our Lord.

>Thankfully,
>Chip Doster

This story reminds me of several Scriptures. In Ephesians
4, Paul discusses how the gifts of the Spirit that each
believer receives from God should be used for the good
of the whole body. Verses 15–16 say, "Speaking the
truth in love, we are to grow up in all aspects into Him
who is the head, even Christ, from whom the whole
body being fitted and held together by what every
joint supplies, according to the proper working of each
individual part, causes the growth of the body for the
building up of itself in love."

When everyone serves in the church according to
their gifting, all the needs of the saints are met and
those outside observe and are attracted. Chip's story is
a good example of many members of the church being
obedient in the continual use of their gifts and being
used by God to encourage his faith during his long,
two-year wait.

God also used many people and circumstances to
speak to him and to show him the path He intended
for him to follow. We can trust God who loves us and
guides our lives. He doesn't say He "might," He says,
"I *will* instruct you and teach you in the way which you
should go; I *will* counsel you with My eye upon you"
(Psalm 32:8; italics added).

Another important point is that Chip stayed close
to God as he waited for the answer to his prayers; he

obviously continued attending church and Bible study and looked for God's assurances that He was working. God allowed the long period of time for Chip's good. He grew in his faith and God got the glory through His faithfulness to provide the job where Chip could influence more people for Christ. Chip's motives were pure as he was willing to be wherever God wanted him to work.

Relationships

Whether at home, at school, or at work, there will no doubt be people to interact with as you go through your daily life. I heard someone say, "I love my job except for the people I work with." We cannot always choose who we will work next to or who will be in our family or in our classes, but we can ask God for the grace to be salt and light wherever He places us.

You may be praying for yourself in this situation or someone else may ask you to pray for them because they have a difficult person in their life. Try to stay objective, not taking sides. Rather, point them to Scripture and seek God's direction for how He wants them to get along. For example, if the person asking you to pray for him is having problems with a boss, pray Colossians 3:23 for him.

"Father, I pray for _____ to do his work heartily for You rather than worry about his boss's attitude. Father, we thank You that You will reward _____ because in reality, it is You he is serving. Lord, please give _____ joy knowing that he will share in Your inheritance. May _____ be a good witness for You by the kind demeanor that he shows to his boss. Give _____ your grace in this situation."

God may put difficult people in our lives to strengthen our faith and teach us lessons we would not otherwise learn. Pray (for yourself or) that they will be able to see that person through the eyes of Jesus; and ask God to give them the grace to love that difficult person for His sake, out of obedience. God is able to give us a genuine love for the unlovely if we will ask Him to love them through us.

It is an amazing miracle that He can work in our hearts if we are willing. The transformation in our relationship can be enough to draw the lost to ask how the change happened. Flesh cannot do that, but God's Spirit can bring reconciliation and love where strife had been, and He gets the glory.

Our natural tendency is to pray asking God to change the difficult person; in reality, God wants to change our hearts to trust Him more and be His instrument of grace in the situations in which we find ourselves. Remember God is working in us to make us more like Jesus. Philippians 2:3 is a good reminder about relationships and how to pray. "Do nothing from selfishness or empty conceit, but with humility of mind regard one another as more important than yourselves."

Health and Healing

Jesus spent much of His earthly ministry healing the sick and lame, and He continues to heal people in our day. He gave us direction for asking for healing in James 5:14–15, "Is anyone among you sick? Then he must call for the elders of the church and they are to pray over him, anointing him with oil in the name of the Lord; and the prayer offered in faith will restore the one who is sick, and the Lord will raise him up." Notice the phrase, "the prayer offered in faith." Do you believe God will heal you or the one you are praying for? Jesus did not heal all of the sick people in His ministry on earth and He doesn't heal everyone today, but that is up to Him. It is required of us to pray in faith believing that He can and He will. We can trust Him with the results because He knows best.

We saw some amazing accounts of healing miracles through the church's 24-hour prayer room; because only God could have accomplished them, they gave Him great glory. The doctors were astonished, for instance, by a case where a man was diagnosed with a cancerous tumor that, clearly present on medical tests, had to be removed by surgery. As we prayed fervently for his healing, he went into surgery and had one last test to confirm the location of the tumor. The tumor that was there just weeks before was nowhere to be found. The doctor compared the two screens and could not explain how it could have disappeared. When the family told him that the church was praying, he wanted to know more. That seems to be the reason for healing—glory to God and as a witness to those who need the Savior.

Sometimes the patient is the best witness by the way he or she handles a serious illness with grace. Medical staffs and others around seem confounded by the peace a patient exhibits and want to know what he or she has that they don't. We cannot see the big picture, so when we pray, we need to ask God for healing or for strength for the patient to endure. Either way, people will be drawn to Christ.

When a fellow Christian asks you to pray, the last thing they need is a pity party about their illness or the illness of their loved one. What they need is reassurance that God is in control and that He is aware of their situation. They need encouragement that they will get through the suffering and that God has a purpose in allowing them to suffer. Be faithful to pray and let them know you are praying for them to stand firm through this test.

God causes or allows trials or illness to come into our lives for different reasons. Some reasons are: a result of sin, to get our attention for instruction, or to use it for His glory. We can pray confidently for God to use this difficulty in the way He intends.

In Psalm 23:2 we learn, "He makes me lie down in green pastures; He leads me beside quiet waters." God will often use illness to "make us lie down" to get our attention back on Him where it belongs. We can trust Him with our health and be thankful that He is the Great Physician on our case.

Safety and Good Judgment

A big part of praying for law enforcement officers, fire-fighters, and for anyone in harm's way is praying for their safety and good judgment in their normal, daily work experiences. Military men and women are especially in need of this kind of prayer. In many large cities, the daily commute motivates us to pray for safety and good judgment to stay alive on the highway.

A good Scripture in praying for safety is Psalm 91, personalizing it to the person for whom you are praying. For example, using verse 5, you could pray, "Father, I lift up Captain Jones and ask that he trust in You to remove any fear of the terror in the night or the anticipated roadside bombs that fall around him during trips on dangerous roads. Keep him close to You and give him your peace as he seeks refuge in You. I thank You for Your wings of protection and that You are the One who delivers us from evil."

Praying for Others

Those in authority

In 1 Timothy 2:1–4, we are given specific instructions to pray for those in authority and given the reasons why we should do that. Read the verses, then we will look at what we can learn from them. "First of all, then, I urge that entreaties and prayers, petitions and thanksgivings, be made on behalf of all men, for kings and all who are in authority, so that we may lead a tranquil and quiet life in all godliness and dignity. This is good and acceptable in the sight of God our Savior, who desires all men to be saved and to come to the knowledge of the truth."

In order to lead tranquil and quiet lives, we need to pray for those in authority. That includes both governmental, elected officials and spiritual leaders in the churches and denominations. We are to pray for everyone, believers and unbelievers, those we know and those we don't know. Everyone everywhere needs to be prayed for by name. Why? It is good and acceptable in the sight of God and the biggest and most assuring reason is that He desires for all men to be saved. "Men" in this case stands for mankind, including both men and women.

If your church does not have a list of elected officials, you can visit www.USA.gov to obtain national, state, and local information. Praying through the church membership directory is a good way to be sure to pray for everyone in the church by name; and using a phone book, a whole town can be covered by prayer as it is divided among a group of intercessors. Talk with others at your church to discuss how you might begin to pray intentionally for "all men" in your area.

Pastor and other church leaders

There are many reasons to pray for your pastor, and I encourage you to give him the gift of prayer. Paul continually asked the early church, "Brethren, pray for us!" (See Ephesians 6:19; Colossians 4:3; 1 Thessalonians 5:25; 2 Thessalonians 3:1.) Paul asked them to pray for him to have boldness to speak the gospel clearly so it could be understood, and also for a door to be opened for the preaching of the Word. These are important areas to pray for your pastor, but pray also for his physical needs, his family's health and well-being, for his energy and enthusiasm in leading your church. Pray for intercessors to be called out by God to pray for him daily. If your church does not already have a plan to pray for the pastor and other staff members, visit www.namb.net/prayer for resources that you can use to pray biblically for him.

Missionaries

Missionaries, whether they serve in your city or around the world, need prayer support. There are many demands on their time and the expectations placed on them can become overwhelming. We need to pray that they stay close to the Lord, that they keep their love relationship with Him strong as they seek to serve Him. Missionaries need prayer for their relationships with people they work with or encounter in ministry. We can pray for their daily needs to be met and for financial support for the ministry they are doing.

The man or woman at home who prays often has as much to do with the effectiveness of the missionary on the field, and consequently with the results of his labors, as the missionary himself. In *The Message*, 2 Corinthians 1:11 says, "You and your prayers are a part of the rescue operation—I don't want you in the dark about that either. I can see your faces even now, lifted in praise for God's deliverance of us, a rescue in which your prayers played such a crucial part." The following guidelines can be helpful in praying biblically for missionaries.

- Pray that more people will be obedient to God's call to be missionaries. See Matthew 9:37–38 and 28:19–20.
- Pray for the missionary's own relationship with God, that he or she will continue to grow spiritually and be nourished by the Word. See Ephesians 1:15–23 and Philippians 1:9–11.
- Pray for the missionary's personal needs: health, safety, family relationships, friends, and encouragement. See Psalm 91:1–4, 11.
- Pray for the missionary to clearly communicate the gospel and have boldness in witnessing. See Ephesians 6:19 and Colossians 4:4.
- Pray for the lost to hear the gospel, to repent and believe in the Lord Jesus Christ. See Romans 10:9–10, 13 and 2 Peter 3:9.
- Pray for the missionary's acceptance by co-workers and unity in the body of Christ. See John 17:21 and Romans 15:31.
- Pray for extension of the missionary's ministry and fruitfulness in spiritual endeavors. See Colossians 4:2–3 and 2 Thessalonians 3:1.

Salvation for the Lost

Only God can save a soul, and each person must decide individually if he or she will believe in Jesus and accept the free gift of salvation. Prayer is an important part of the process. Here are a few suggested ways to pray:

- Plead for the person you are praying for as God's purchased possession in the name of Jesus and on the basis of His shed blood. "In Him we have redemption through His blood" (Ephesians 1:7).
- Ask God to tear down the works of Satan, like false doctrine, unbelief, or other teaching that the enemy may have built up in the person's life. Pray for his thoughts to be taken "captive to the obedience of Christ" (2 Corinthians 10:5).
- Pray that the Holy Spirit will convict him of his sin and his need for a Savior. "The kindness of God leads you to repentance" (Romans 2:4).
- Pray that the person will hear, receive, or read God's Word and that God's will and purposes may be accomplished through Scripture. "So will My word be which goes forth from My mouth; it will not return to Me empty, without accomplishing what I desire" (Isaiah 55:11).
- Pray that the person's eyes will be opened and ears unstopped so that the truth is heard. "And even if our gospel is veiled, it is veiled to those who are perishing, in whose case the god of this world has blinded the minds of the unbelieving so that they might not see the light of the gospel of the glory of Christ" (2 Corinthians 4:3–4).
- Pray with consistency and perseverance, not to persuade God but because of the resistance of the enemy (read Daniel 10:12–13). "Therefore, my beloved brethren, be steadfast, immovable, always abounding in the work of the Lord, knowing that your toil is not in vain in the Lord" (1 Corinthians 15:58).
- Thank God for making us more than conquerors. "But in all these things we overwhelmingly conquer

through Him who loved us" (Romans 8:37). "But thanks be to God, who gives us the victory through our Lord Jesus Christ" (1 Corinthians 15:57).

Other Christians

Paul gives many examples of prayers for fellow Christians, and it is a good exercise to pray Scripture to learn how to pray for those you know and love as well as members in a church membership directory. Using Colossians 1:9–12 you could pray this way.

> Father, You know that I want to be faithful to pray for _____ and to ask You, Lord, to fill _____ with the knowledge of Your will in all spiritual wisdom and understanding, so that he will walk in a manner worthy of You, Lord, to please You in all respects. Father, I pray that _____ will bear fruit in every good work and increase in knowledge of You; strengthen him with all power according to Your glorious might. Give him steadfastness and patience that he might give You thanks because You qualified us to share in the inheritance of the saints in Light.

Ephesians 1:15–19; 3:14–19; and Philippians 1:3–11 are also prayers that Paul prayed for the early saints, and are well suited to learning to pray biblically for other Christians. The more you pray Scripture, you will begin to find yourself incorporating these same phrases and attitudes in your prayers when you're not looking at the Bible.

There is Scripture to pray for any category of person—husband, wife, child, teacher, medical staff, and the list goes on. When praying for yourself or

others, let the Bible be your guide and ask the Holy
Spirit to fill you to overflowing so that you can pray in
the character of Jesus; then give God the glory when He
answers your prayers.

I pray for you, dear reader, to be given from God a
spirit of wisdom and of revelation in the knowledge of
Jesus Christ. I pray that the eyes of your heart may be
enlightened, so that you will know the hope of God's
calling, the riches of the glory of His inheritance in the
saints, and what is the surpassing greatness of God's
power toward us who believe. In Jesus's name, amen.

══════ **Review** ══════

1. What are some questions we can ask ourselves to
   distinguish between needs and wants? _____

   _____

   _____

2. What is a good Scripture to memorize related to our
   jobs or career concerns? _____

   _____

3. How do we pray for difficult people we may find in
   our lives? _____

   _____

4. What are some things to keep in mind when someone asks us to pray for a person who is ill, facing
   surgery, or has some medical problem?_____

   _____

   _____

5. What are three reasons God may bring or allow illness in our lives? _____.

   _____ , _____

6. Why does God instruct us to pray for those in authority and for all men? _____

   _____

7. Are you praying for your pastor? _____ Will you make a commitment to pray for him? _____

   _____

CHAPTER 7

Spiritual Warfare in Prayer

I remember like it was yesterday, marching around the room in children's church at the chapel on Johnson Air Force Base in Japan. We were the children of army and air force fathers, so pretending to be soldiers was very familiar. We would march around while we sang "Onward, Christian Soldiers." If you are not familiar with the song, just read the words below.

"Onward, Christian Soldiers"

1. Onward, Christian soldiers, marching as to war, with the cross of Jesus going on before! Christ, the royal Master leads against the foe; forward into battle see His banners go!

Chorus

Onward, ye soldiers, marching as to war, with the cross of Jesus going on before.

2. At the sign of triumph Satan's host doth flee; on, then, Christian soldiers, on to victory! Hell's foundations quiver at the shout of praise; brothers, lift your voices, loud your anthems raise!

3. Like a mighty army moves the church of God; brothers, we are treading where the saints have trod. We are not divided, all one body we—one in hope and doctrine, one in charity.

4. Onward, then, ye people, join our happy throng; blend with ours your voices in the triumph song. Glory, laud and honor unto Christ the King, this thru countless ages men and angels sing.

(Words: Sabine Baring-Gould in Church Times, 1865, Public Domain)

The words in this hymn are instructive, and contain sound doctrine based on 2 Corinthians 2:14, "But thanks be to God, who always leads us in His triumph in Christ, and manifests through us the sweet aroma of the knowledge of Him in every place."

Jesus leads us into the battle against the foe. It is our praise of His triumph that causes the devil to flee. The line of the Christian is offense, not just defense. Our tactic is to storm the gates of hell with our praise of Jesus. He has already won the victory over sin and death. Our goal is setting captives free!

Another vital element highlighted in this great hymn is that our charge as Christians is unity—we are not divided. That was paramount in Jesus's mind as He prayed to His Father just before His crucifixion. In John 17:21 Jesus prayed, "That they may all be one, even as You, Father, are in Me, and I in You, that they also may be in Us, so that the world may believe that You sent Me."

He wanted us to be perfected in unity. How it grieves our Father when we as Christians can't seem to get along with other Christians, since we are all in His family and He wants us to love one another.

Wear the Right Uniform

Men and women in the military wear the uniform of their branch of the service. Whether they are in—the army, air force, navy, or marines can easily be distinguished by their uniforms. We as Christian soldiers have a uniform that not only identifies us but also protects us from our enemy. This is not your typical uniform.

In Ephesians 6:10–19 we read, "Finally be strong in the Lord, and in the strength of His might. Put on the full armor of God, so that you will be able to stand firm against the schemes of the devil. For our struggle is not against flesh and blood, but against the rulers, against the powers, against the world forces of this darkness, against the spiritual forces of wickedness in the heavenly places. Therefore, take up the full armor of God, so that you will be able to resist in the evil day, and having done everything, to stand firm.

"Stand firm therefore, having girded your loins with truth and having put on the breastplate of righteousness, and having shod your feet with the preparation of the gospel of peace; in addition to all, taking up the shield of faith with which you will be able to extinguish all the flaming arrows of the evil one. And take the helmet of salvation, and the sword of the Spirit, which is the word of God. With all prayer and petition pray at all times in the Spirit, and with this in view, be on the alert with all perseverance and petition for all the saints, and pray on my behalf, that utterance may be given to me in the opening of my mouth, to make known with boldness the mystery of the gospel."

Gird your loins with truth

Many people use this Scripture daily as a reminder to put on the armor. While the armor is available to every Christian, we may not be appropriating the power and protection provided. How do we gird our loins with truth? It is often pictured as a wide belt of truth in the uniform or whole armor.

As used in Scripture, the phrase "gird up your loins" means to get ready to do something difficult or strenuous. Jesus Christ is truth; His word is truth, so we need to know Jesus and His word to be prepared for the battle. In Nahum 2:1 God says, "The one who scatters has come up against you. Man the fortress, watch the road; strengthen your back [loins], summon all your strength."

We are called to be people of integrity, not only believing God's word is true but living by it and telling the truth in all areas of our lives. Satan is a liar and the father of lies and his primary target is our mind. He likes to sprinkle in some truth with his lies so it sounds right to us. Be alert by immersing your mind with God's word of truth.

Peter exhorts us in 1 Peter 1:13, "Prepare your minds for action, keep sober in spirit, fix your hope completely on the grace to be brought to you at the revelation of Jesus Christ."

Put on the breastplate of righteousness

We acquire righteousness through the shed blood of Jesus when we entrust our life to Him. When God looks at us, He sees Jesus and His righteousness is imputed to us. Recognizing our position in Christ is so important because our accuser will try to remind us of forgiven sin.

Memorize Romans 8:1 and stand firm and courageous. "Therefore there is now no condemnation for those who are in Christ Jesus." We also need to stay in healthy condition with God; meaning that any new sins are confessed and we are being obedient to Him. Confess as soon as conviction of sin arises.

T. W. Hunt said when he feels convicted and asks for forgiveness, he prays, "That was not like You, Jesus, and I want to be like You." Psalm 119:40 says, "Behold I long for Your precepts; revive me through Your righteousness."

We have power over our enemy when we are walking in right relationship with our heavenly Father. Likewise, unconfessed sin gives our enemy an advantage. Paul reminds us in Ephesians 4:25–32 of the importance of a clean life and exhorts us in verse 27, "Do not give the devil an opportunity.

Bill Bright also emphasized the importance of keeping short accounts with God. He called this spiritual breathing—exhale by confessing sin and inhale by receiving a fresh filling of the Holy Spirit. Breathe deeply!

Shod your feet with the preparation of the gospel of peace

Not only are we to live in peace with others (Romans 12:18) and rest in the promise of God's peace (Philippians 4:6–7), we are to be prepared to share the good news of Jesus Christ. As Peter tells us in 1 Peter 3:15, "But sanctify Christ as Lord in your hearts, always being ready to make a defense to everyone who asks you to give an account for the hope that is in you, yet with gentleness and reverence."

Take up the shield of faith

This vital element of the uniform is to protect us from the flaming missiles of thoughts and feelings that Satan shoots at us. Recognize these misleading thoughts by their content. If they try to get you to doubt God or to rationalize why you should disobey Him, they are from the enemy. Jesus said to Peter in Matthew 16:23, "Get behind me, Satan! You are a stumbling block to Me; for you are not setting your mind on God's interests but man's."

Make it a practice to "seek first God's kingdom and His righteousness" so as to avoid a lot of problems. Flaming missiles of the evil one are extinguished by our faith in Jesus Christ. In 1 John 5:4 we read, "For whatever is born of God overcomes the world; and this is the victory that has overcome the world—our faith."

Take the helmet of salvation

When we come to Christ, our bondage to Satan is broken and our salvation is secure. However, we must resist the devil's attempts to entrap us. Paul says in Philippians 2:12–13, "Work out your salvation with fear and trembling; for it is God who is at work in you, both to will and to work for His good pleasure." In order to live a life of peace, a life pleasing and useful to God, we must be diligent in having our minds transformed (Romans 12:1–2) and turning loose of "the sins which so easily entangle us" (Hebrews 12:1).

First Thessalonians 5:8 says, "But since we are of the day, let us be sober, having put on the breastplate of faith and love, and as a helmet, the hope of salvation." The old hymn "Blessed Assurance" comes to mind when I think of our hope of salvation. We do have assurance that Jesus is ours and we belong to Him, and that gives us a taste of what is to come when we see Him face-to-face—glory divine!

Take up the sword of the Spirit

Just as Jesus used Scripture to resist the devil's temptations, we are to hide God's word in our heart that we might not sin against Him. (See "Memorizing Scripture" in appendix.) His word is powerful and doesn't return to Him void. Knowing the word is important, so that we can resist a specific sin or thought with a specific Scripture. In Hebrews 4:12 we are assured, "For the word of God is living and active and sharper than any two-edged sword, and piercing as far as the division of soul and spirit, of both joints and marrow, and able to judge the thoughts and intentions of the heart."

What a uniform! Don't leave home without it. Take off the old self (Colossians 3:1–10) and put on God's righteousness (Colossians 3:12–17). Thank God for protecting us and preparing us to succeed in our battle with the powers of darkness.

Know Your Enemy

When going into war, it is important to know about the enemy. Learning about his strengths, weaknesses, and where he is vulnerable helps us plan to win the war. A successful football coach will also scout out his opposing team to learn all he can about the competition for the next big game.

Knowing strengths and weaknesses is important whether in war or in sports. It is also important to us in living the Christian life. Once we ask Jesus into our heart, we are an enemy of the devil. Being in the war is not optional. That's why we are instructed to put on the whole armor of God so that we can resist the devil. We can learn all we need to know about our enemy in the Bible.

In Ephesians 6:12 we see that the devil is a schemer and devious, trying to find our weakness. There will be struggles in the Christian walk. Jesus forewarned us in John 16:33, "These things I have spoken to you, so that in Me you may have peace. In the world you have tribulation, but take courage; I have overcome the world." Peter reminds us to be alert to our enemy in 1 Peter 5:8, "Be of sober spirit, be on the alert. Your adversary, the devil, prowls around like a roaring lion, seeking someone to devour."

Remember how the serpent (devil) created doubt in Eve's mind by saying, "Indeed, has God said, 'You shall not eat from any tree of the garden'?" (Genesis 3:1). He led her to rationalize the right to disobey. In Revelation 12:7–12, the war between Michael and his angels against the dragon and his angels is described. Verse 9 says, "And the great dragon was thrown down, the serpent of old who is called the devil and Satan, who deceives the whole world." And verse 10 says, "The accuser of our brethren has been thrown down, he who accuses them before our God day and night." In verse 12 we are assured that "he has only a short time."

In China, an American missionary was consoling a Chinese Christian about the enemy they had in the Communist government. The Chinese man said, "It is easy to know our enemy because we can see him. I pray for you Americans, as you cannot see your enemy who is subtly destroying your country."

Ours is a decline rather like a frog being boiled in water without jumping out. The water starts out cold and gradually warms up. As we think how tolerant of sin all around us we in the church have become, it's easier to understand why God required the children of Israel to utterly destroy their enemies. The foreign gods would contaminate His chosen people and He was intolerant of sin. (See an example in Joshua 6–7.)

We have hope, however. In Revelation 12:11, we recognize our strength against the devil as the blood of Jesus, "And they overcame him because of the blood of the Lamb and because of the word of their testimony, and they did not love their life even when faced with death." The old hymn "There Is Power in the Blood" is right on target. The devil doesn't stand a chance, but he will try to convince us that he does and continue to try to trip us up.

In *Webster's* dictionary, the word *devil* is defined as "diabolus, slanderous, to slander, lit. throw across, see ball." The mental picture of the devil throwing a ball between Christ and us or between us and a fellow Christian can help us to be alert to his devious tactics.

He is always trying to divide Christians and too often we see each other as enemies instead of recognizing his tactics. He is tricky, "But thanks be to God, who always leads us in triumph in Christ, and manifests through us the sweet aroma of the knowledge of Him in every place" (2 Corinthians 2:14).

More important than spending too much time getting to know about the devil is to spend time getting to know God and the power He has given to us through Christ Jesus. In Romans 16:19 God through Paul says, "But I want you to be wise in what is good, and inno-cent in what is evil."

Bank tellers being trained to recognize counterfeit bills are given genuine bills to study closely. Because they know the genuine so well, a counterfeit is easy to spot. The better we know the Word of God, the easier it will be for us to spot the tricks of the devil that are usually wrapped in some of God's truth.

Remember when the devil tried to tempt Jesus, he used Scripture. We need to know the whole truth! "Beloved, do not believe every spirit, but test the spirits to see whether they are from God, because many false prophets have gone out into the world" (1 John 4:1).

Know Why You're on the Battlefield

In Japan our family would often take car trips to explore the countryside. The dirt roads were not too bad unless an oncoming car stirred up a dust storm. Without air-conditioning we rode with the windows down. When Daddy saw an oncoming car, he would call out, "Man your battle stations!" We would each roll up our window as fast as we could to miss the dust. I understood what he meant and knew what to do when he gave the command.

While I was driving over to South Carolina one Saturday to speak in a church the next morning, I was listening to a Gamecocks football game. I heard the announcer say more than once that the player on the field seemed to be confused about what he should do with the ball. That reminded me of verses 18–19 of Ephesians 6. We got all dressed up in our armor of God; now what are we supposed to do?

We are to pray in the Spirit and be alert. We are to pray for fellow believers, especially for those who are sharing the gospel. We are to persevere in prayer, not just say a quick, quiet prayer. Prayer is work. We are trying to set captives free and the enemy doesn't want to turn them loose.

This kind of prayer requires a sacrifice of our time, sometimes our food and sleep too. When God awakens you in the night with someone's name on your mind, ask Him how He wants you to pray and stay in prayer for that person until He gives you the peace to stop.

When He knows He can count on you to obey His promptings, He will enlist you to pray the prayers that He wants prayed to accomplish His good pleasure. Your prayer may be for someone's protection or salvation. What a blessing to be a soldier in God's army. Are you prepared for battle?

> "Now [Jesus] was telling them a parable to show that at all times they ought to pray and not to lose heart."
>
> —Luke 18:1

> "We have the idea that prayer is for special times, but we have to put on the Armor of God for the continual practice of prayer, so that any struggling onslaught of the powers of darkness cannot touch the position of prayer."
>
> Oswald Chambers

═══ **Review** ═══

1. What causes the devil to flee? _____

_____

2. What could happen if Christians were not divided?

_____

_____

Is there anyone you need to contact to be reconciled? _____ Will you take action? _____

3. Can you name and describe the pieces of the full armor of God? _____

_____

_____

4. Why is it important to stay righteous before God?

_____

5. How can we recognize thoughts that are coming from the devil? _____

6. What does it mean to transform our minds and why is it important? _____

_____

7. What does Revelation 12:11 say is our strength against the evil one? _____

8. Where can we learn all we need to know about our enemy? _____

9. What are we supposed to do after we put on the armor of God? _____

10. Why is it important to know the truth of God's Word? _____

_____

CHAPTER 8

Putting Prayer into Action

I'm glad that you have chosen to read this book on prayer, but now it is time to take action steps to move from theory into prayer as a lifestyle. There are some specific steps you can take to grow into the prayer relationship you are seeking with our Lord. Like any other goal, there needs to be a plan of action to see any change. For balanced growth, it is beneficial to pray alone with God, to join with others nearby to pray corporately, and to connect with national initiatives.

Personal Prayer Activities

We talked about developing a personal quiet time in chapter 2, so we won't repeat that here. It is good, however, to consider additional ways to strengthen your personal prayer life. The following is not exhaustive, but it is offered as a few suggestions to get you thinking. The following ideas—a prayer retreat with God, a prayerwalk, and praying for a public servant or elected official—are personal prayer activities where you can begin acting out your faithfulness in God.

Prayer retreat

Rather like a vacation to spend time with your family, a personal prayer retreat can give you rest and enrich your relationship with your heavenly Father. A good place to start is with a few hours in isolation away from cell phones, computers, and other people. Turn loose of all other concerns as you would have to do if you were in a meeting, or taking someone to the doctor. Read the Twenty-third Psalm and reflect on your Good Shepherd. Meditate on His words there, "He restores my soul." It may be beneficial to play some prayerful, worshipful music to calm your mind and spirit.

Read your Bible like a love letter from the Lover of your soul. Read until you feel led to stop, then meditate on what got your attention. Write out the verse and talk to God about it. What is He telling you? Are you seeking His wisdom for a big decision? Are you being convicted of sins from which you should repent? See "Scriptures for Confession of Sin" in the appendix for a beginning list of verses to consider related to sin. (See Psalm 19:12–13.)

As you read the Scriptures and ask yourself questions related to them, the Holy Spirit may bring things to mind that you have overlooked. We can easily become tolerant of "socially acceptable" sins, but God is a holy God and He is calling us to be holy. Make a list of every sin that He brings to your mind, both those committed and sins of omission, and confess them. It is important not only to confess sins but also to turn loose of them—to repent.

Repent means to stop going in the wrong direction and make a change to go in the right direction. After you have allowed God to "create in [you] a new heart," make a ritual of burning your paper with the sins written on it, to demonstrate to yourself that they are forgiven and forgotten by God. Read 1 John 1:9 and receive restoration that only comes from our Lord.

A weekend away at a hotel or cabin can give you a chance to totally unwind from the pace of everyday life and focus on getting to know God better. In addition to the ideas on the previous page for use of your time, consider some practical issues of a longer retreat. Make plans for getting away with God so that you won't be concerned with responsibilities for work or family. Even with the best-made plans, you can expect some transition time from busyness to total focus on God and your relationship with Him. If you are fasting, drink plenty of water and take a nap when you become drowsy. Relax in the presence of your Lord. Your retreat is for both physical and spiritual renewal.

Vary your setting depending on your location and the weather. For example, take a prayerwalk in the woods, sit reflectively in a park to take in the beauty God created. How long has it been since you noticed, *really* noticed, the variety of flora—the trees, plants, and flowers—or wildlife like birds, ducks, geese, squirrels, or the mountains or the ocean waves? Let Him know how much you enjoy His handiwork and praise Him for the majesty before you. If you are not normally an early riser, set your alarm to get up to enjoy the sunrise with the One who set it in motion. There's nothing like enjoying the sunset with our Creator, giving full attention to His handiwork to see how beautifully and quickly it changes.

A time of confession and repentance is important in a retreat of any length. As God convicts your heart, write down your commitment for changes that you need to make. Spend some time asking God to examine your motives for Christian activity. Are you overcommitted to impress others with how "spiritual" you are? Are you making deals in your mind with God to buy His favor? God does not call us to do every activity at church or to serve in all ministries at once. He does call us to use our gifts for His glory and for the building up of the body of Christ. (See Ephesians 4:11–16.) If what you are doing is simply a task, it may well be something that God did not call you to do. What God directs, He blesses.

The other extreme may be your issue. Are you failing to participate for fear of not being good enough or talented enough? When God calls you to do something, He will also equip you and that can be very freeing—to know all you have to do is be obedient.

Allow the preceding ideas to trigger your thinking toward other creative ways to spend extended time with God, and make it a habit to "get away from it all" on retreat with Him. He is calling you in Mark 6:31 to "come away by yourselves to a secluded place and rest a while."

Prayerwalking 101

Do you feel like you have two left feet when it comes to prayerwalking? Here are a few tips to help you get off on the right foot.

Pray for Direction. Prayer originates with God, so talk with Him about how to get started, "Call to me and I will answer you" (Jeremiah 33:3), and where He would have you walk and pray. "Your ears will hear a voice behind you saying, 'This is the way, walk in it'" (Isaiah 30:21). Think of prayerwalking as a way to get to know God better by taking a walk with Him.

Get Cleaned Up. Before you can pray for others, you need to be in right relationship with God. Allow the Holy Spirit time to examine your heart, confess any known sin, and accept God's forgiveness. Then you will be a clean vessel ready for God's use in prayer. "Search me, O God, and know my heart" (Psalm 139:23–24). "If we confess our sins, he is faithful and just and will forgive us our sins and purify us from all unrighteousness (1 John 1:9).

Get Dressed. The object of a prayerwalk is not to draw undue attention to yourself, so it's best to leave the monk's robe and incense-box-on-a-rope at home. In addition to putting on the whole armor of God as described in Ephesians 6:10-18, wear clothing appropriate for the season and location (culture) along with comfortable walking shoes.

Start Where You Are. Don't worry about whether you do everything just right, or what other people may think of you, "Do not fear the reproach of men" (Isaiah 51: 7). Lean on the Holy Spirit. "In the same way, the Spirit helps us in our weakness" (Romans 8:26–27).

Take a brief walk around your neighborhood asking God to give you eyes to see your neighbors as He sees them. Pray silently for them as God gives you insight about them from bikes, boats, or other items you see.

Use Scripture. To keep your prayers biblical, spend time reading the Bible. Memorize God's Word; or carry a few key verses on index cards to refer to as you pray. "So is my word that goes out from my mouth: it will not return to me empty, but will accomplish what I desire and achieve the purpose for which I sent it (Isaiah 55:11).

Thank God that He loves your lost neighbors and pray that they would believe in Jesus (John 3:16). Ask Him to bring them out of darkness (Colossians 1:13–14). Pray for them to be released from whatever hinders their faith" (2 Timothy 2:25–26). Allow God to teach you through Scripture to pray in the character of Jesus, and remember "[God] is able to do immeasurably more than all we ask or imagine" (Ephesians 3:20), so pray believing He will answer.

Involve Others. Invite a Christian friend at work to come to work early to walk by each desk and pray for fellow workers. Think about places you'd like to prayer-walk and Christians you know in that setting who might walk and pray with you. Participate in organized prayerwalks at your church or in your community. The best way to learn to prayerwalk is to give it a try; so tie your shoes and take those first steps while you're thinking about it.

Shield-a-Badge

The Shield-a-Badge-with-Prayer movement has grown without ownership from any organization. The ministry involves individuals praying daily for public servants such as law enforcement officers and firefighters in their communities or military men and women. Anyone who wears a badge—such as school crossing guards, security guards, and others—could also be included.

After the September 11, 2001, attacks on the World Trade Center in New York City, many individuals became impressed by God to pray for those who work in harm's way to provide the rest of us security at home. Some things to pray for include wisdom, good judgment, protection, and a safe return home. If this interests you, ask your pastor or your church prayer coordinator if your church has an organized Shield-a-Badge ministry.

However, whether or not your church has an organized ministry to pray for public servants, you can pray daily for police officers, firefighters and our military personnel. Visit www.namb.net/prayer and look under free resources for an overview of this kind of ministry. You may sense God calling you to take the lead for such a ministry in your church.

Elected officials

You may be interested in praying for a specific elected official in your personal prayertime. The National Day of Prayer Task Force offers an Adopt-a-Leader kit to help you be effective in your endeavor. You can visit www.nationaldayofprayer.org to obtain a kit.

Praying with Other Christians

There is a great benefit to praying with other Christians, especially if they are more mature in their faith or further along the spiritual path. We retain what we are learning about prayer by putting it into practice. "Iron sharpens iron, so one man sharpens another" (Proverbs 27:17). There is power in agreement in prayer too. Are there opportunities in your church to participate in prayer groups? Visit Wednesday night prayer meeting, if your church offers one, to get a taste of praying in a group.

You can enlist a prayer partner, join a telephone or email prayer chain, participate in a prayer group for a variety of interests, serve in a 24/7 prayer room, or agree in prayer with a national initiative.

Prayer partner or mentor

When I was young in my faith, I was in a Bible study and took seriously the suggestion to enlist a prayer partner. I asked a more mature Christian woman to pray with me on a weekly basis. I was blessed to have her for a mentor prayer partner. We met together to pray each week, and I could sense that I was in the presence of the Lord when we prayed.

I grew in my prayer life as I was exposed to what to pray and different ways to pray. For example, one week she called me and said, "My schedule is too full for us to get together, so let's pray over the telephone." I gasped, "Can you do that? Does that count?" I had never prayed over the phone before so I was being stretched. Now, years later, I automatically offer to pray with most callers. I became more confident and comfortable praying with others because of that experience of being mentored.

If you are just beginning to pray, ask God to bring a mentor into your life to help you grow in your prayer life. Look around for a more mature believer or ask your pastor to suggest someone who would be a good mentor. The more you pray with another person or in small groups, the more comfortable you will become praying in a group and in agreement with others. Jesus said in teaching the disciples how to pray, that they should pray this way: "Our Father." This indicates that we should pray together with others in the family of God.

Prayer chains

When our church was a mission church, we had two prayer chains to help us pray for one another's needs. The women's prayer chain was a great experience for me as I grew in praying with others on the phone. The following is a sample of instructions for a prayer chain participant that may help you determine if you would like to be a part of a prayer chain.

One of the most important things to remember is that all prayer requests are confidential, and they should be passed to the next person just the way you received them, verbatim if possible. It is helpful to use a notebook of some kind to document all incoming prayer requests. You can use blue or black ink to write the prayer requests on one side of the paper and leave room to write the answer when it comes, in red ink. As the notebook becomes full, the red will stand out and increase your faith that God does indeed answer prayer.

It will be important to know how prayer requests may be added to your prayer chain and who you are to call if you have a prayer request. Try to make your request as concise as possible to make it easy for participants to pass it along throughout the chain.

When you receive a call, write down the request and call the next person on the list. Pass on the exact information that was given to you. Don't edit or add information. Be careful not to gossip about prayer requests. Trustworthiness is an important characteristic of prayer chain participants.

If you get no answer, keep calling down the list until someone answers to keep the chain going. You may back up later to inform those who didn't answer if you have the opportunity, but it is not necessary. It is very helpful for the last person in each group to call his or her captain to verify that the requests have been received.

Immediately after making the call, pray for the prayer requests. Try not to leave your phone until you have prayed, so that you don't become involved in other things before you pray. You may also pray with the person giving you the message and with the one you call. Pray for God's will and pray fervently as instructed in James 5:16*b*: you can be the instrument that moves the hand of God.

If you find that you are repeatedly unavailable to receive the phone calls or you decide you no longer desire to be a part of the prayer chain, let the chairperson of the chain know. A prayer chain is only as strong as the weakest link, but it can be a rich blessing and very effective when it functions as God's instrument.

Many former telephone prayer chains have changed to email prayer chains so that the exact request can be forwarded. Confidentiality is just as important with an email prayer chain as it is with the telephone prayer chain.

Prayer groups

Does fear of what to say in prayer hold you back from participating in a prayer group? Jesus told the disciples before sending them out, "Do not worry about how or what you are to say; for it will be given you in that hour what you are to say. For it is not you who speak, but it is the Spirit of your Father who speaks in you" (Matthew 10:19–20).

Times of corporate prayer can help us as individuals in the body of Christ grow into His likeness, so why are so many people nervous about it? One reason is fear of not praying "right." It can be fear of what other people will think if we get tongue-tied, stutter, or worse—don't know the right terminology of prayer. Public prayer is talking to God who loves us, in agreement with others, so we can relax in God's presence.

Agreement in prayer

Praying with others in a group always includes Jesus; and for that reason, those times can be some of the most meaningful experiences in our prayer lives. God's power is released through agreement in prayer. Jesus said in Matthew 18:19–20, "Again I say to you, that if two of you agree on earth about anything that they may ask, it shall be done for them by My Father who is in heaven. For where two or three have gathered together in My name, I am there in their midst."

In order to agree in prayer, though, everyone must be able to hear each other. We need to listen well and pray loud enough for others to understand us. It is best to pray short, simple, and specific prayers. This is not the time to try to impress other people with your deep theological knowledge. Clear and to the point is best for group agreement. Praying shorter and specific prayers allows the Holy Spirit to prompt people to pray something in agreement with what was just prayed.

For example, if the topic is to pray for our pastor, one may pray for his sermon preparation, another for his health. If the floor is open long enough on the topic of our pastor, someone may think to pray for him to be able to attend his daughter's ballgame that is important to her. No one person knows all there is to pray about on any given topic. Silence can be good, as God wants to be a part of our conversation with Him and this allows the Holy Spirit to prompt us to pray what is on the heart of God.

If prayers get too long or the subject is changed several times, it can quench the Holy Spirit. Jesus said, "And when you pray, do not keep on babbling like pagans, for they think they will be heard because of their many words" (Matthew 6:7 NIV). Imagine we are praying, and when you mention the upcoming outreach event, I feel prompted to pray for an aspect of the event that you haven't mentioned. However, I can't get a word in and you continue to pray and change the subject several times. By the time I can pray, I have forgotten what I felt prompted to pray. Remember short and simple is good in group prayer. You can pray more than once or interject an agreeing word.

Allow God to speak

It is helpful to have your Bible with you when you are praying in a group as the Holy Spirit may prompt you to read a passage of Scripture that applies to the subject being prayed over. Prayer can be a dialogue with our Father, so when you feel prompted to read a particular verse, it may be a word from Him that will be edifying to the group.

Submit to the Holy Spirit when you come to the place of prayer whether praying alone or in a group; and ask Him for His perspective on the situation you are praying about. Seek God's glory and you can be assured that you will be praying in the will of your Father.

So often in prayer, we do all the talking and even in groups someone is usually speaking. When the Holy Spirit gives us nothing to pray for a few moments, we should get excited because He may be ready to speak what is on the heart of God. We sure don't want to miss what God has to say, so don't rush to fill the void if silence occurs.

Dependence on God is a key

Since it is God calling us to pray aloud the prayers He puts on our hearts, we can relax and just obey Him. Lean heavily on the Holy Spirit, especially when you are not sure what to say. Remember the encouraging promise from Romans 8:26 (NIV), "In the same way, the Spirit helps us in our weakness. We do not know what we ought to pray for, but the Spirit himself intercedes for us with groans that words cannot express." It is so good to know that even if we mess up the words, God sees our hearts and knows our deepest thoughts.

I've heard T. W. Hunt say about our position in praying—that the Holy Spirit has us by one hand as He indwells us and Jesus has us by the other hand as He is at the right hand of God—so we're in pretty good company when we pray! A three-strand cord is not easily broken either. (See Ecclesiastes 4:12*b*.)

God meets us at our point of need when we are participating in a prayer group. Stepping out on faith to do something new or uncomfortable in our walk with the Lord can be scary, but when we "will" to obey, God equips us for the task. When our hearts are sincere, the Holy Spirit gives us what we need to be ourselves and express our prayers in a natural way.

Public confession of sin

Any time we come into God's presence, we can expect to be convicted of sin in our lives, so it is important to discuss what needs to be confessed publicly. If you have done something to offend the whole church or the prayer group, then you should confess to the large group. But if the sin is not public, it should not be confessed to the large group.

This is especially true if anyone else was involved with your sin. If you offended one person, go to that one person to ask forgiveness along with asking God to forgive you. Think about whether anyone would be hurt unnecessarily by a public confession; if so, that would be reason enough to keep the confidence between you and your heavenly Father.

There are times when a public confession can turn into a stumbling block for someone else. Too many graphic details can be tantalizing to an unsuspecting soul and take the focus off of Jesus who forgives and restores us to righteousness.

However, confession of shortcomings before a group has been known to be a catalyst for revival with other people becoming convicted of prayerlessness, or greed, or envy, or some other sin common to man. Honesty in a group builds trust and integrity before God and that's a good setting for conviction. Anything confessed publicly should be kept confidential and turned over to God in prayer for the person who is confessing.

Sunday morning worship prayer group

Many churches have a group that meets on Sunday morning for the purpose of praying for the ongoing worship service. If your church offers this opportunity, give it a try. Some of the things to pray for during the worship include prayer for boldness of the preacher to speak the truth in love and to seek to please God rather than man. It is good to pray for attendees to be released from any strongholds that may have a hold on their lives. Pray for decisions that need to be made about trusting Christ or to commit one's life to full-time Christian service. Pray against distractions that are trying to destroy the work of the Holy Spirit in the hearts of the people in the congregation.

The order of worship or Sunday bulletin can be used as a guide to know what will be happening and who will be leading the worship. Pray for the worship leader, the choir or musicians, anyone sharing a testimony or leading in prayer. Ask God to be in control of the worship service and the prayertime on its behalf.

Neighborhood prayer groups

Your neighborhood may have a prayer group that you can visit or join. However, if you can't find an existing group, you can start one by prayerwalking your neighborhood streets to pray for your neighbors. Then as God leads, knock on doors to ask if anyone is interested in joining a prayer group. If they are not, ask if they have a prayer request that the group can pray for. Most people will give a request and that gives you a reason to go back to get an update.

As you pray, opportunities to share the love of Christ will be revealed. It has been amazing how God has opened doors in some areas and redeemed lives because of the prayer effort by two or three faithful ones. The national lighthouse of prayer movement is an excellent way to reach neighborhoods for Christ. The concept is easy and very effective. You can enlist your family, co-workers or fellow students to commit to a threefold ministry to pray, care for, and share Christ with your neighbors, business associates, or class mates.

Specific focus prayer groups
Where there is an interest, there can be a prayer group. It may be missions; focused prayer for the church—ministers, activities, outreach, members; or civic affairs including current bills up for voting; or education and schools—principals, teachers, students, and curriculum. If you have an interest and there's no active group that you can find, you may be the one who needs to invite others to pray with you about your interest or concern.

Triplets
This is a wonderful way to pray for your lost relatives or friends while enjoying accountability and support from two other people. Triplets by their name obviously mean that you would invite two friends to meet with you weekly for the purpose of praying for each other, as

well as three friends each that you want Jesus to save. Whether it is friends in your neighborhood, your office, or a school, it is good to choose people that are in close proximity on a regular basis so you can pray for the total of nine people.

It has been supernatural how when I have been in a triplet praying for someone, I suddenly see that person more frequently, have natural conversations and favor when I try to share my faith. God really does honor our faithfulness to pray what is on His heart—salvation of souls.

Prayer Room

What happens during an hour?

If your church has a prayer room, you may wonder what goes on there. Many churches have a prayer room that is accessible only to intercessors that have made a commitment to serve there on a regular basis. The prayer requests that are submitted to be prayed over in the prayer room are confidential, so often it is kept locked. God leads different churches to set different policies and tailor the systems for organizing prayer rooms to their situation. However, there are similarities that are worth mentioning here.

Typically you as a church member will make a commitment for a set period of time, such as a year, to go to the prayer room on the same day and at the same time on a weekly basis to pray for the prayer requests organized there. Categories for prayer may include some or all of the following:

- Church membership list
- Names of and requests from pastor and other staff members

- List of deacons, elders, Bible study teachers, and chairpersons of ministry teams
- Elected officials
- Schools with principals' names
- Missionaries' names and requests
- Sanctuary pew prayer request cards and telephone prayer request cards

That list may seem overwhelming, but you are not expected to pray for every request. All of the categories will have some recognizable signal for where to begin praying and how to let the next person also know where to begin. It may be a simple bookmark-type divider saying, *Start here.*

As any prayer ministry grows, the number of prayer requests will also increase, which explains why there is a system in place to know where to start and how to move from category to category. Perhaps there's a salvation board containing different names for each week, a bulletin board to highlight urgent prayer requests, or a thank-you notes board to share cards received from those being prayed for. A good plan is to spend about ten minutes each in five different categories, and before leaving allow time to praise God for the many answers on an answered-prayer board.

If you are the intercessor scheduled to serve, you would show up at the prayer room just moments before your hour begins, so that you don't disturb the intercessor who is praying before you. A brief greeting is exchanged and then they are gone. Sign in the attendance book next to your hour.

Ask the Holy Spirit to be in control of your time and the prayers that you pray. Then before settling into the desk chair, look at the urgent board and pray for those life-and-death prayer requests and for the names on the salvation board.

Try to pray for at least one request in most of the categories to help ensure that all requests get prayed for continually. As you feel prompted by the Holy Spirit, write a note of encouragement to someone that you are praying for to let them know you are praying.

So many people write that they are amazed when people who don't even know them are praying for them. Even a nonbeliever appreciates kind thoughts of them when they are sick or in the hospital, and that thoughtfulness could lead to their interest in knowing more about what we believe.

As you pray for fellow church members, you may also want to write a note to let them know you prayed for them. Many church members find out about the prayer ministry in the church because of receiving a note from an intercessor. It's amazing, too, how often the notes "just happen" to arrive when they need a lift.

Sometimes God prompts us to be the answer to another Christian's prayer before he even prays. God is in control of the prayer room, so just report in for duty and be blessed to be a part of all that He wants to do through you.

Telephone guidelines

The telephone is the link between those with needs and the intercessor. Your voice and manner will be the only contact some people will have with your church and the prayer room. Answer the phone with the agreed upon greeting, maybe something like, "_____ church prayerline. God answers prayer, may I help you?" A greeting signifying that this is a prayerline helps the caller know he or she dialed correctly and gives him or her a moment to be sure what he or she wants to say.

Express interest and concern for the caller and listen to what he or she says. It is helpful to have a note pad handy to write a few notes as the caller talks. As a natural part of your conversation, try to find out if he or she knows Jesus as Savior. The person is calling for prayer and for that reason we can know he or she has some interest in spiritual things, even if he or she doesn't know Him. It is a good question to help find out if you are talking with a church member or someone who got the phone number from a promotion of some kind. If the caller shows interest in knowing more about Jesus, you can share the good news naturally as you are able or you could even read a gospel tract to him or her.

Testimony of sharing a gospel tract

One time in the early days of our prayer ministry when I was the coordinator, I was in my office that was adjacent to the prayer room when the phone rang. With no intercessor in the room, I ran over and answered the telephone.

The caller on the phone said, "I have just lost my job because my job was dependent upon my being a student and I've been put on probation because of my grades. My wife told me if I lost my job, she was leaving me." I said, "Whew, I sure hope you know Jesus!"

Now that was not the way I taught intercessors to respond to calls and I'm not sure why I said that so suddenly, but I did. There was a long pause, then he said, "I'm not sure . . . can you tell me about Him?"

My heart started racing and thoughts ran through my mind, "I know Jesus, I love Jesus, I should be able to tell him about Jesus." But for some reason, I felt tongue-tied. Thankfully, we had stocked the desk drawer with gospel tracts and I quickly opened the drawer to get one out. I asked him if I could read a few verses from the Bible and he said yes, so I began to read the tract.

As I read, I would check with the caller to see if what I was saying made sense, or if he had questions. He stayed with me, and when we got to the part where I asked him if he would like to pray and invite Jesus into his heart, he said, "You know, I think that's exactly what I need to do. My mother has been praying for me all my life."

I almost fell over, because I knew the caller's decision had nothing to do with my ability to share the gospel; it was God at work over the telephone. I led him through the sinner's prayer and got very excited as he invited Jesus into his heart. Then I started asking if he had a Bible and where he lived so we could get him involved in a nearby church.

After we talked a while longer, I asked him if he would like to pray again and thank God for what He had just done in his life and for what He was going to do. After another long pause, he prayed, "Dear God, I want to thank You for that billboard with this phone number on it, so I could call and this lady could tell me about You and Your love for me."

I really got choked up, since I had been very concerned about using billboards to advertise the prayerline phone number. Billboards are very expensive, and I thought the perception would be that we were wasting the tithes entrusted to our church. I had been overruled in the vote and I had not had a peace about it.

God is so good; He not only saved the dear man who called, but at the same time He clarified to me that if we will get the phone number out to the public, He will use it to draw people who need to know Him to call. If we are willing to be available, He can use us for His glory.

Dealing with fear

Trusting and obeying God are vital to responding to His call to serve in a prayer room. Even when you are called by God to pray there and you want to obey, it is easy to be paralyzed by fear. It is an act of faith, trusting that God will truly equip us to do what He is calling us to do. Our response is an act of the will.

In preparation for a "Call Out of Intercessors" to serve in the prayer room, one year we arranged for a skit to illustrate fears people have about serving. The young man walked onto the stage muttering to himself, "I know I said I'd serve in the prayer room, God. I want to obey You, but well, I . . . I've seen people go into the prayer room (long pause, then quickly), but I've never seen them come out!" As he got closer to the door, he finally got up enough courage to go inside where there was a huge, oversized telephone. He immediately began to pray that God would keep the phone from ringing.

Apparently the skit struck a nerve because people began to admit that they would like to serve in the prayer room but did not feel ready to answer the phone. It helped bring that fear out into the open so we could deal with it.

There is life after answering the prayer room phone

Danette Rhodes volunteered to help me update prayer requests and work in my office, but she didn't feel *qualified* to answer the phone. Each time she would come to help, the conversation would always get back to her being afraid to answer the prayerline phone.

She would admit, and anyone who knows her would agree, that she is neither a shy person nor particularly afraid to talk to people. It was just that this was so, so spiritual. It is spiritual. The prayer room belongs to God; and if we are trusting and available, the Holy Spirit can speak through us and give us the words to say.

Because my office was adjacent to the prayer room, if the phone rang and there was no intercessor, I would run to answer the phone. That would happen from time to time when she was there. She would hear me as I talked to whoever called.

One day when Danette was working in my office, I was on my telephone and the phone in the prayer room rang with no intercessor in there. Well, she knew instinctively that it must be answered and I was tied up. Oh my! With tremendous fear and trepidation, she walked slowly to the phone; it kept ringing. She finally got up her nerve and answered the phone.

When she floated back into my office, I looked up into the biggest smile I had ever seen on her face. She was radiant and exuberant. "I did it, I did it!" She exclaimed as she told me word for word what had been said. God had indeed been gracious and given her what she needed to handle the call and pray over the phone! She was a new intercessor.

God is in control

It is interesting how many times the intercessor answering the phone could relate to the caller. Maybe they had experienced the same situation, or they used to be plagued with the same besetting sin and had seen God have the victory in their life. The natural empathy that flows in that scenario is wonderful. It is an illustration of 2 Corinthians 1:3–5, "Blessed be the God and Father of our Lord Jesus Christ, the Father of mercies and God of all comfort who comforts us in all our affliction so that we will be able to comfort those who are in any affliction with the comfort with which we ourselves are comforted by God."

Another day when I was working in my office, with no intercessor next door in the prayer room, the phone rang and I ran to answer it. This was to be an exception to the rule. I really could not relate to what the gentleman was telling me. As a part of the training, intercessors are encouraged to pray, asking for a fresh filling of the Holy Spirit. The idea is to relinquish control and let the Lord be in control of all that goes on during the hour of prayer.

While the man was talking, I was praying, "Lord, this call is for You! What should I say to this man?" I was praying and listening, and also flipping pages in the open Bible on the desk. I know it didn't really do so, but it seemed like a verse jumped out at me. It wasn't a verse I would have noticed in my own Bible with all the notes and underlining. It wasn't even a verse I was familiar with.

When the man on the phone took a breath, I asked him if I could read a verse to him from the Bible. After a pause, he cautiously almost questioningly said, "Yes." When I read the verse to him, the man began to weep. He finally said, "That is just what I needed to hear." Then I got choked up and said, "Well, that was from God." I confessed to him, "I really didn't know what to say to you, so I asked God what to say, and that was the verse God gave me for you." I prayed with him thanking and praising God for His all-sufficiency in meeting both of our needs. Now it was my turn to float out of the prayer room.

More telephone guidelines

A typical phone call to the prayer room is from someone who is familiar with the system, and they will quickly give you the prayer request and expect you to offer to pray with them before you hang up. While you are on the phone, take a few notes to get the information straight, so that when you hang up, you can record the request on a prayer card for others to see.

Offer to pray with every caller, including staff members. Give your first name only if asked and never give your or any intercessor's home phone number. Try to obtain the name and address of the person being prayed for so that a note of encouragement can be sent. Try also to get the phone number of the caller so that follow-up can be made for an update.

Writing notes of encouragement to callers

If a printed or purchased notecard is available, it is good to go ahead and write a note to let the person know you are praying. If the caller was asking for prayer for himself, you could note in your card that you were glad to talk with him and the intercessors will continue to pray for him. Keep in mind that your note needs to be uplifting and encouraging, not judgmental.

When you feel prompted to write a note but you're not sure what to say, writing Scripture out with a reference is a good idea. God's Word does not return to Him void. You can look in a Bible promise book, provided in the room, for a verse that relates to the caller's situation. It is amazing how God will give many different people the same verse to send to the same person and the Scripture impacts that person. God's Word is active and alive; only He can orchestrate those kinds of "coincidences."

Frequent callers

Most of the calls to the prayer room are for specific requests and can be handled in a brief amount of time. However, when lonely people find out that there is a number they can call and have someone kind to talk to, they will call often.

You can recognize this kind of caller by the fact that they have no specific prayer request, they just want to talk. It's important to show compassion and God's love to these frequent and sometimes difficult callers.

Be a good listener to get general information, and then as soon as possible, bring the conversation to prayer. Ask, "How may I pray for you today?" If they continue to ramble, say, "Let me pray for you," and pray using what you have heard about their situation. After praying, let them know they may call back as often as they need to and that you will make a note of their call so that other intercessors can also pray for them.

Let them know you care about them, but that you have a guideline of keeping calls brief. Give the disclaimer that intercessors are not counselors but are here to pray. Politely but firmly let them know you must hang up to return to praying for the requests there.

Difficult callers

Occasionally, someone who is angry—in general or specifically at God—will call. Do not take the caller's comments personally or argue with the caller. Remember Proverbs 15:1, "A gentle answer turns away wrath, but a harsh word stirs up anger." If a caller refuses to agree to your offer to pray over the phone for him, tell them that you will pray for him when you hang up. If a caller becomes obscene, hang up immediately and pray for him.

Though rare, there may be a caller who wants personal information about you or another intercessor. Tell him that we are all here on behalf of our church to pray for those who call. Turn the conversation back to finding out how you may pray for him. If it becomes obvious that he is just trying to develop a relationship, tell him you must hang up and that you will pray for him. Avoid becoming personally involved with any caller.

Praying with National and International Initiatives

Even if your church offers few opportunities to pray with others at this point, you can pray in agreement with national initiatives. The following is just a short list to give you an idea.

National Day of Prayer

The National Day of Prayer (NDOP) is officially the first Thursday in May every year. If your church does not know about or observe this day, here are some suggestions. Invite a friend or two to join you on that day to pray together or find a large event in your area.

Ask your pastor if this could be used for a catalyst to call your church members to come together for corporate prayer for our nation. He could call a few other churches and consider inviting the community. Since it is a day enacted by law, many people who will not attend church will come to a patriotic call to prayer. There may be a NDOP chairperson in your city or state to help your church get started. Visit www.nationaldayofprayer.org for more information and/or to find an event near you. Information about Adopt-a-Leader, which is praying for a specific elected official, can also be obtained from the NDOP Web site.

See You at the Pole

See You at the Pole (SYATP) primarily involves students, who join with others around the world by meeting, before classes begin, at their school flag pole for prayer with fellow Christian students in September. It is a way for Christian students to stand up for their beliefs and to bolster support for one another as they live out their faith on their school campuses. Learn more at www.syatp.com.

You can be involved by promoting SYATP and encouraging discussion about it among youth in your church. There have been many churches that have enlisted adults to prayerwalk the school campuses prior to the beginning of school in late summer. The night before See You at the Pole would be another good time to organize a prayerwalk.

Moms in Touch International

Moms in Touch International (MITI) has as its goal one group of praying moms for every school in the world. Moms in Touch is simply mothers of children in the same school meeting together each week to pray for their children and their children's school. To find a group near you, visit www.MomsInTouch.org.

You may also visit the National Prayer Committee Web site to find contact information for many more national prayer initiatives that you as an individual can participate with. Visit www.nationalprayer.org.

> "You can do more than pray after you have prayed, but you cannot do more than pray until you have prayed."
>
> A. J. Gordon

Review

1. What can you do to achieve balanced growth in prayer? _____
   _____

2. Why should we consider going on a prayer retreat alone with God? _____
   _____

3. What is usually needed when we spend extended time with God? _____
   _____

4. Have you ever been on a prayerwalk? _____
   Where are some places that would be good to prayerwalk? _____
   _____

5. Who besides police officers could benefit from a focused prayer approach? _____
   _____

6. Are you currently in a prayer group? _____.
   Why should we pray with others? _____
   _____
   _____
   _____
   _____

7. What is the guideline for public confession of sin?

_____

_____

_____

_____

_____

8. Do you have to be in a prayer room to pray with someone over the telephone? _____. Is praying over the phone something you do now or would be willing to try? _____

_____

9. What specific action will you take as a result of reading or studying this book? _____

_____

Conclusion

Somewhere along the way, the church has been lulled to sleep in complacency, rather than staying alert and ready for action—very much like a sleeping giant. However, we are called to be a mighty army of God, on the offense against our enemy. Jesus said, "I will build My church and the *gates of Hades* will not overpower it" (Matthew 16:18; italics added).

Gates by their very nature are defensive edifices, designed to keep intruders out. There has been a misconception about us being only on the defense against the deceptions of the evil one. While it is important to be alert to the devil's tactics, we need to be moving into his territory of darkness with the Light of the world, knowing that his gates cannot stop us!

Prayer is preparation for sharing the good news of freedom for the captives to sin and death. Our role as intercessors is integral to reclaiming the earth, working with our Savior to redeem a lost world. You and your believing prayers are essential to the turnaround.

As you become equipped to pray through practice and become more aware of the importance of your prayers, like Elijah you can be a part of the reversal of our downward spiral further and further into decadence. You can also influence those around you to join the movement of prayer. We can link arms with intercessors around the world like highways on a map and bring the power of God to earth as it is in heaven.

Put Prayer into Practice

The best way to learn to pray is to practice praying on a regular basis, alone and with others. Start where you are, thinking of your interests. What are you passionate about? Pray about that, and ask God to give you a hunger and thirst for more of Him. Ask Him to help you find others to pray with too. Spend time in His Word and pray it back to Him. We learn by doing, so don't just read and talk about prayer, Pray! It is my prayer that you will develop such a love relationship with our Father that you will pray without ceasing as a lifestyle.

> "Prayer honors God, acknowledges His being, exalts His power, adores His providence, secures His aid . . . to pray really, to pray till hell feels the ponderous stroke, to pray till the iron gates of difficulty are opened, till the mountains of obstacles are removed, till the mists are exhaled and the clouds lifted, and the sunshine of a cloudless day brightens—this is hard work, but it is God's work and man's best labor."
>
> E. M. Bounds

Appendix 1

Answers to Review Questions

Chapter 1

1. What are ten reasons to pray? *God chose to love us and communicate with us through prayer; we are His ambassadors (and need to report in); to imitate Jesus who is at the right hand of the Father making intercession for us; God is searching for an intercessor; biblical examples; Jesus taught us to pray; love for God; to get direction for living; obedience to God; protection from evil.*

2. Name four relationships we have with God. We are His *children,* we are His *friends,* we are His *priests,* and we are His *fellow workers.* In which role do you feel most comfortable and why?

3. What are some sacrifices we are called to make as God's priests? Sacrifice of *thanksgiving,* sacrifice of *our bodies,* sacrifice of *good stewardship,* sacrifice of *praise.* What does holy living look like and why is it costly?

4. What kind of fellow workers is God looking for? *Obedient ones.*

5. What makes God listen to our prayers? *God initiates prayer; He is training us for eternity; He invites us to pray; we pray according to His will, praying for His glory, when we come with clean hearts.*

6. What hinders our prayers? *Sin, wrong motives, and unbelief.* Why is forgiveness of others so important? *Jesus said to be reconciled to our brother before we come to Him.*

7. How can we experience the joy of our salvation? *Confess sin, repent, and accept forgiveness.*

8. What are three analogies God uses to tell us that he forgets our forgiven sins? *He washes away our sins; He puts them behind His back; and He casts them into the sea.* Another good answer: *Sins are scarlet but will be white as snow.*

9. What is the goal of prayer? *Maturity.*

10. Prayer is God's plan for accomplishing His purposes. Will you be one He can depend on to pray?

Chapter 2

1. What is the primary reason you pray? *This should be your personal answer.*
   Do you think of prayer as building a love relationship with God?

2. Name three helpful tools to keep handy in your place of personal worship.
   Bible, pen, and paper.

3. What are good reasons for memorizing Scripture? *It will be available for the Holy Spirit to prompt us to use in resisting temptation or sharing our faith; God's Word is truth and truth will set us free; and "All Scripture is inspired by God and profitable for teaching, for reproof, for correction, for training in righteousness; so that the man of God may be adequate, equipped for every good work" (2 Timothy 3:16–17).*
   Which verse will you memorize first?

4. When circumstances seem to overwhelm us, what is the best thing to do? *Focus on God, and praise Him.*

5. What does fasting with prayer demonstrate? *Humility before God, dependence on God, teaches our bodies to obey the Spirit, priority we give to prayer, and the seriousness of our desire for the outcome.*

Chapter 3

1. Why is it good to begin prayer with praise or adoration? *Jesus taught disciples to pray that way; we become like what we worship; draws us closer to Jesus; will help us know what our objective is in becoming more Christlike; and it helps us see our need for confession.*

2. What gives us the right to talk to our Abba (Father)? *Adoption as children of God.*

3. And without *faith* it is impossible to please Him.

175

4. An important purpose of prayer is *building a relationship with God.*

5. The priority of prayer is *the will of God.*

6. What does it mean to take every thought captive to the obedience of Christ? *By an act of our will we can decide to obey God and not dwell on thoughts that would lead us into sin.*

7. What is the difference between praise and thanksgiving? *We praise God for who He is and we thank Him for what He has done.*

8. Do you think using the alphabet to learn the names of God will help you get to know Him better?

_____

How will you use it?

Chapter 4

1. What is the phrase that Jesus often used about listening? *"He who has ears to hear, let him hear."*

2. What are some ways we may hear God? *Through His Word, through the Holy Spirit, and through others.*

3. What does waiting on God help us learn? *To rest in God's promises.*

4. What are three ways God answers prayer? *Yes, no, and wait.*

5. Why does God answer our prayers with no? *The request is not His will, He is protecting us from harm that we can't see.*

6. What is the danger we need to avoid when God answers yes? *Taking God for granted or thinking He didn't have anything to do with the answer.*

7. Why did God give us commands? *To keep us from stumbling (See John 16:1).*

8. What does God expect us to do when we hear His command? *Obey Him.*

Chapter 5

1. How can prayer be a pleasure? *Get to know God, grow in relationship, and obey Him.*

2. What is the secret for receiving God's peace that passes all understanding? *Be anxious for nothing, but in everything by prayer with thanksgiving tell God what is on your heart.*

3. Name the eight things to focus our minds on in Philippians 4:8. *Whatever is true, whatever is honorable, whatever is right, whatever is pure, whatever is lovely, whatever is of good repute, if there is any excellence, anything worthy of praise.*

4. How can we get a glimpse of God's glory? *Mature by practicing our faith and studying God's Word, and when we see a life changed in a radical way.*

5. What are some of the benefits of keeping a journal? *Solidifies our memory of God's faithfulness, builds our faith, expresses thanks to God, gives God the glory, leaves a legacy, clarifies our thoughts, imparts understanding and insight; it's therapeutic; it's exciting; and it prepares us to share with others.*

6. Do you keep a journal? _____. What is your favorite reason?

Chapter 6

1. What are some questions we can ask ourselves to distinguish between needs and wants? *Will what we are seeking bring God glory? What is our motive? Can we be content with little or generous to bless others if we prosper?*

2. What is a good Scripture to memorize related to our jobs or career concerns? *Deuteronomy 8:18, "You shall remember the Lord your God, for it is He who is giving you power to make wealth."*

3. How do we pray for difficult people we may find in our lives? *Pray to be able to see the person through the eyes of Jesus; ask for grace to love the difficult person for God's glory; and offer your will to love the person if God will empower you to do so.*

4. What are some things to keep in mind when someone asks us to pray for a person who is ill, facing surgery, or has some medical problem? *They don't need a pity party; reassure the person that God is in control; pray for strength of the sick person to stand firm in their*

faith as a good witness; pray for person to draw close to God; and ask God to heal their bodies for His glory.

5. What are three reasons God may bring or allow illness in our lives? *A result of sin, to get our attention for instruction, or to use it for His glory. Or all three.*

6. Why does God instruct us to pray for those in authority and for all men? *To lead a quiet and tranquil life, it is good and acceptable in sight of God, and He desires for all men to be saved.*

7. Are you praying for your pastor? _____ Will you make a commitment to pray for him?

Chapter 7

1. What causes the devil to flee? *Our praise of the triumph of Jesus on the Cross.*

2. What could happen if Christians were not divided? *The world might more easily believe that God sent Jesus into the world as our Savior.*
   Is there anyone you need to contact to be reconciled? _____. Will you take action?

3. Can you name and describe the pieces of the full armor of God? *The belt of truth—knowing the truth and being truthful; breastplate of righteousness—clean before God; shoes of peace—live in peace with others and be prepared to share good news of Jesus; shield of faith—trusting God and setting mind on His interests; helmet of salvation—security in Jesus as we study His Word to transform our minds and resist sin.*

4. Why is it important to stay righteous before God? *We have power over our enemy when we are in a right relationship with our heavenly Father.*

5. How can we recognize thoughts that are coming from the devil? *By the content, trying to get us to doubt God or rationalize why we should disobey Him.*

6. What does it mean to transform our minds and why is it important? *Fill our minds with God's word and thoughts of Him to take every thought captive to obedience of Christ.*

7. What does Revelation 12:11 say is our strength against the evil one? *The blood of Jesus Christ.*

8. Where can we learn all we need to know about our enemy? *In the Bible.*

9. What are we supposed to do after we put on the armor of God? *Pray in the Spirit and be alert.*

10. Why is it important to know the truth of God's word? *It will be easier to spot the tricks of the devil that are usually wrapped in some of God's truth.*

Chapter 8

1. What can you do to achieve balanced growth in prayer? *It is beneficial to pray alone, to join with others to pray corporately, and to connect with national initiatives.*

2. Why should we consider going on a prayer retreat alone with God? *It can give you rest and enrich your relationship with your heavenly Father.*

3. What is usually needed when we spend extended time with God? *A time of confession and repentance.*

4. Have you ever been on a prayerwalk? _____. Where are some places that would be good to prayerwalk? *Neighborhood, office or workplace, school, church.*

5. Who besides police officers could benefit from a focused prayer approach? *Firefighters, military men and women, security guards, school crossing guards, and elected officials.*

6. Are you currently in a prayer group? _____. Why should we pray with others? *God's power is released through agreement in prayer; learn from those who are more mature in their spiritual walk; put into practice what we are learning about prayer; iron sharpens iron.*

7. What is the guideline for public confession of sin? *If you have done something to offend the whole church or the prayer group, then you should confess to the large group. But if the sin is not public, it should not be confessed to the large group. If your public confession of sin would hurt another person needlessly or become a stumbling block for others, it should not be confessed publicly.*

8. Do you have to be in a prayer room to pray with someone over the telephone? *No.* Is praying over the phone something you do now or would be willing to try? _____

9. What specific action will you take as a result of reading or studying this book? _____

_____

Appendix 2

Scriptures for Confession of Sin

God's word is "alive and active and sharper than a two-edged sword" so it is good to look into Scripture and ask God to bring to your attention any overlooked sin that you need to confess. The following is a short list of such Scriptures. I encourage you to compile your own list and use it often.

Renew Your Mind

Romans 12:1–2: "Therefore I urge you brethren, by the mercies of God, to present your bodies a living and holy sacrifice, acceptable to God, which is your spiritual service of worship. And do not be conformed to this world, but be transformed by the renewing of your mind." Are you focusing on God's word above TV, radio, cell phone, computer, and other attention grabbers? Does your life look more like the world or like Christ?

Prayer as Lifestyle

1 Thessalonians 5:17: "Pray without ceasing." And Psalm 5:3: "In the morning, O Lord, You will hear my voice; in the morning, I will order my prayer to You and eagerly watch." Do you have a regular time to read your Bible and talk with God? How often are you aware of His presence with you in your daily routine? Do you talk to God about everything or only in a crisis?

Judgmental Attitude

Matthew 7:1–2: Jesus says, "Do not judge so that you will not be judged, for in the way you judge, you will be judged." What is Jesus saying to you? How does this apply to your life? Ask God to examine your heart to see if you have a judgmental attitude that you are unaware of and ask Him to change your heart to please Him.

Forgetfulness

Psalm 77:11: "I shall remember the deeds of the Lord; surely I will remember Your wonders of old." Do you know the biblical wonders that God performed? Are you aware of God's activity all around you today? Do you remember how great God is and talk about Him with others?

Scripture Memory

Psalm 119:11: "Your word I have treasured in my heart, that I may not sin against You." Are you making an effort to memorize Scripture?

Sin of Omission

James 4:17: "Therefore, to one who knows the right thing to do and does not do it, to him it is sin." Was there a kindness you could have shown, but you didn't? Are you hoarding the spiritual gifts God has given you to use for edification of the body?

Use of Money

Malachi 3:8: "Will a man rob God? Yet you are robbing Me! But you say, 'How have we robbed You?' In tithes and offerings." Do you know that God owns everything and we are His stewards? Does that affect how you use your money? Do you give a tithe of your income to support God's work in your church first?

Jealousy and Selfish Ambition

James 3:16: "For where jealousy and selfish ambition exist, there is disorder and every evil thing." Do you want what others have? Are you envious of attention shown to someone else? Do you feel left out? Are you striving to get ahead at all costs? What are your motives for your hard work?

Use of Your Tongue—Speech

James 3:5: "So also the tongue is a small part of the body, and yet it boasts of great things." Does your speech please your heavenly Father? Do you check to make sure what you are saying is true? Do you struggle with gossip?

Appendix 3
Memorizing Scripture

Scripture that is stored in our memory is available for God to use at the right times in our lives. The Holy Spirit can prompt us to use Scripture in resisting temptation and in situations of sharing our faith. If you think it is something you cannot do, reflect for a few minutes about how many commercials from radio or TV that you remember quite easily. It is the repetition that makes it stick with you. Ask God to empower you to remember His Word so that you can get to know His commands to obey and promises to stand on.

Memory Exercise

Writing out Scripture can help us retain it. Try this method. Leave out some key words to see if you can fill them in. Start out with the whole verse on a whiteboard or computer screen. Read it through several times. Erase a few key words and read it through again. Do you remember the missing words? Great, now erase a few more until all you have left is the reference. It is important to review verses that you have memorized.

You might even enlist an accountability partner to help you both learn and retain more of God's Word. Repeat the verses often to keep them correct and fresh in your mind. It is a good practice to say the reference for where the verse is found in the Bible at the beginning and the end of the verse.

The following are some verses that I recommend for memorizing.

God's Priority For Prayer
Matthew 6:33: "But seek first His kingdom and His righteousness, and all these things will be added to you."

Forgiveness of Sin
1 John 1:9: "If we confess our sins, He is faithful and righteous to forgive us our sins and to cleanse us from all unrighteousness."

Value of Scripture
2 Timothy 3:16–17: "All Scripture is inspired by God and profitable for teaching, for reproof, for correction, for training in righteousness; so that the man of God may be adequate, equipped for every good work."

Word of God Is Living
Hebrews 4:12: "For the word of God is living and active and sharper than any two-edged sword, and piercing as far as the division of soul and spirit, of both joints and marrow, and able to judge the thoughts and intentions of the heart."

Renew Your Mind

Romans 12:1–2: "Therefore I urge you, brethren, by the mercies of God, to present your bodies a living sacrifice, acceptable to God, which is your spiritual service of worship. And do not be conformed to this world, but be transformed by the renewing of your mind, so that you may prove what the will of God is, that which is good and acceptable and perfect."

God Hears and Answers Prayer

1 John 5:14–15: "This is the confidence which we have before Him, that, if we ask anything according to His will, He hears us. And if we know that He hears us in whatever we ask, we know that we have the requests which we have asked from Him."

Holy Spirit Helps Us Pray

Romans 8:26 (NIV): "In the same way, the Spirit helps us in our weakness. We do not know what we ought to pray for, but the Spirit himself intercedes for us with groans that words cannot express."

Fruit Bearing

John 15:7–8: "If you abide in Me, and My words abide in you, ask whatever you wish, and it will be done for you. My Father is glorified by this, that you bear much fruit, and so prove to be My disciples."

God Is Able

Ephesians 3:20–21: "Now to Him who is able to do far more abundantly beyond all that we ask or think, according to the power that works within us, to Him be the glory in the church and in Christ Jesus to all generations forever and ever. Amen."

Resist Temptation

1 Corinthians 10:13: "No temptation has overtaken you but such as is common to man; and God is faithful, who will not allow you to be tempted beyond what you are able, but with the temptation will provide the way of escape also, that you may be able to endure it."

Test the Spirits

1 John 4:1: "Beloved, do not believe every spirit, but test the spirits to see whether they are from God; because many false prophets have gone out into the world."

Put Away Childish Things

1 Corinthians 13:11: "When I was a child, I used to speak like a child, think like a child, reason like a child; when I became a man, I did away with childish things."

Eternal Security

John 10:28–30: "And I give eternal life to them, and they will never perish; and no one will snatch them out of My hand. My Father, who has given them to Me, is greater than all; and no one is able to snatch them out of the Father's hand. I and the Father are One."

No Condemnation in Christ

Romans 8:1: "Therefore there is now no condemnation for those who are in Christ Jesus."

Sweet Aroma of Christ

2 Corinthians 2:14: "But thanks be to God, who always leads us in triumph in Christ, and manifests through us the sweet aroma of the knowledge of Him in every place."

Also by

Elaine Helms

If My People . . . Pray,
Steps to Effective Church Prayer Ministry

Published by
Church Prayer Ministries
PO Box 71732
Marietta, GA 30007-1732

New Hope® Publishers is a division of WMU®,
an international organization that challenges Christian believers
to understand and be radically involved in God's mission.
For more information about WMU, go to wmu.com.
More information about New Hope books may be found
at NewHopeDigital.com. New Hope books
may be purchased at your local bookstore.

Books to deepen your *walk*

Heart's Cry
Principles of Prayer
Jennifer Kennedy Dean
ISBN-10: 1-59669-095-X
ISBN-13: 978-1-59669-095-0

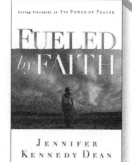

Fueled by Faith
Living Vibrantly in the Power of Prayer
Jennifer Kennedy Dean
ISBN-10: 1-56309-993-4
ISBN-13: 978-1-56309-993-9

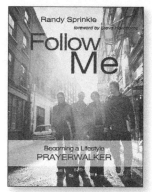

Follow Me
*Becoming a Lifestyle
Prayerwalker*
Randy Sprinkle
ISBN-10: 1-56309-948-9
ISBN-13: 978-1-56309-948-9

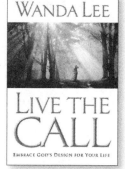

Live the Call
Embrace God's Design for Your Life
Wanda Lee
ISBN-10: 1-56309-994-2
ISBN-13: 978-1-56309-994-6